W9-AZB-204

Chinese Mythology

Chinese Mythology

Anthony Christie

Half-title page. A bronze leaping tiger of the Zhou dynasty. The Chinese associated the tiger with autumn and the west. British Museum, London.

Frontispiece. A mountain and a dragon surmount the bowl of a tripod-based earthenware incense burner from the Yellow Temple, Beijing, Yuan dynasty.

Chinese Mythology first published 1968.
New revised edition published 1983.

This edition published by
Barnes & Noble, Inc.,
by arrangement with
Reed International Books Ltd

1996 Barnes & Noble Books

Library of Congress Cataloging in Publication Data

ISBN 0 7607 0191 1

Produced by Mandarin Offset
Printed in Hong Kong

M 10 9 8 7 6 5 4 3 2 1

Contents

The Chinese Setting

It is hard to grasp the physical extent of the country which we know as China, whose more than three thousand years of written history provide a cultural continuity without parallel. In size China is continental: its area is about the same as Europe's. Its climates range from that of the sub-Arctic taiga of Manchuria to that of the sub-tropical jungles of the south-west. Its terrain is of great diversity: the upland plateau of Tibet, where the high ranges are covered with perpetual snow; the deserts and steppe of Central Asia; the rich deltas of the south-east coast; the great plains of the lower Yellow River valley.

Within this enormous space there is room for a great diversity of peoples and cultures. Nevertheless it is possible to discern a main group which dominates the entire area: it is this group that we call Chinese, and whose culture we have in mind when we talk of China. The various other ethnic groups within the political frontiers of China are almost all mongoloid peoples, as are the Chinese themselves; all have been influenced to a greater or a lesser extent, over the centuries, by the Chinese. But influences have not all flowed in one direction and, historically, what we call Chinese culture is itself the result of millennia of cross-fertilisation among numbers of different groups.

The point in time at which it is possible to identify a given group or aggregation of groups as being the Chinese (in anything approaching the modern sense) is difficult to determine, but it is perhaps reasonable to do so at the moment when the Qin dynasty (221-207 B.C.) brought about the first unification of China. Though this did not last, Qin Shi Huang Di (221-210 B.C.) is thought of as the first Emperor. Under his successors of the Western and Eastern Han dynasties (206 B.C.-A.D. 220) a central government which ruled the whole country became a fact. Centralised government, with minor interruptions, has persisted until the present day. The Qin achievement has not been forgotten, however, and it is from this dynasty that the name China is derived – though the Chinese themselves have always preferred to refer to their country as the Middle Kingdom, Zhongguo. When, about the beginning of the Christian era, news reached the Chinese of a great empire to the west of them – it was in fact that of Imperial Rome – they called it Da Qin after the first great empire in China itself. But although the Han dynasty made China a reality, not all the regions inside today's political frontiers were included in the Han empire, and the country did not achieve its final extent until some centuries later.

Within the geographical space which we now call China there are three-well marked zones. Of these the central one lies about the Huang He, the Yellow River, its main feature. There is every reason to believe that this region was the cradle of the nucleic culture, the core of Chinese civilisation. The zone to the north is that of the great plains of Manchuria, together with the Manchurian uplands and the mountainous regions drained by the Amur River. The mountains are forested, the plains now heavily eroded but once covered with mixed forest. The climate is continental and shows extreme variations. To the south of the Yellow River lies the third zone, which includes the area to the north of Chang Jiang or the Yangtze River up to about the 33rd

Above. This great mound covers the tomb of Qin Shi Huang Di, the emperor who first united China and brought to an end the conflicts of the Warring States period (480–221 B.C.). The tumulus, at Lintong, Shaanxi, beneath Mount Qi, covers a vast underground palace which was begun at the beginning of this reign. It was probably looted shortly after his death by Xiang Yu despite its defences, which included such devices as automatic cross-bows.

Left. The attempt by Qin Shi Huang Di, first unifier of China, to have one of the Nine Cauldrons of Yu hauled out of the Si River. Possession of the cauldrons, like sacrifice on Tai Shan, would confirm the founder of the new dynasty as Son of Heaven; but every time the cauldron reached the surface a dragon bit through the ropes, and the cauldron was lost for ever. Rubbing from a stone relief in the tomb of the Wu family in Shandong. Second century A.D. Musée Guimet, Paris.

parallel, the Yangtze valley and the region to the south with its many rivers and lakes. Its western boundary is marked by the Cinling mountains. Most of this region consists of hills, but there are two other well-defined areas: the Sichuan basin, which is drained by the upper Yangtze; and the plain towards the coast, which is drained by the lower Yangtze and the Huai River, itself a tributary of the Yangtze. Unlike the other two zones, this southern region has ample rainfall, with large areas of sub-tropical and tropical forest. The main crop is rice, whereas in the north the staples are wheat, millet, beans and *gaoliang* (sorghum). The central region, the Chinese homeland, has a temperate climate, with an adequate rainfall. Its western area consists of a loessic highland zone, from which there is a gradual transition to the rich alluvial plains to the east, while the Shandong peninsula forms a third sub-division. The mixed forest cover has been much reduced by human intervention and there is a trend to semi-aridity.

U. S. S. R.
MONGOLIA
HEILONGJIANG
Amur
XINJIANG (autonomous region)
JILIN
GANSU
XIONGNU
NEI MONGOL ZIZHIQU (Inner Mongolia)
LIAONING
NORTH KOREA
Great Wall
Ordos Desert
BEIJING
YEN
Beijing
QINGHAI
ZHAO
SHANXI
HEBEI
Bo Hai Bay
SOUTH KOREA
NINGXIA
Fen He
QI
Anyang
SHANDONG
WEI
LU
YELLOW SEA
SHANG
Huang He/Yellow River
ZHOU
Xi'an
Luoyang
Zhengzhou
SONG
Wei He
Banpo (Panpo)
HAN
JIANGSU
QIN
SHAANXI
HENAN
ANHUI
WU
Qinling Shan
TIBET (Xizang – autonomous region)
SHU
HUBEI
Shanghai
SHANGHAI
CHU
SICHUAN
BA
Jialing
Chang Jiang/Yangtze River
YUE
INDIA
ZHEJIANG
EAST CHINA SEA
Changsha
HUNAN
JIANGXI (autonomous region)
GUIZHOU
FUJIAN
YUNNAN
Shizhaishan
DIAN
GUANGXI
Xi Jiang
TAIWAN
GUANGDONG
NAN YUE
Guangzhou
BURMA
VIETNAM
LAOS
Dongson (Dongoon)
Hainan Dao
SOUTH CHINA SEA
CHU
historical names
PHILIPPINE ISLANDS
THAILAND

The Early Cultures

Important evidence for human evolutionary history in China was first found in the 1920s from the limestone exposures at Zhoukoutian some 30 miles (50 kilometres) south of Beijing. There skulls and long bones of a fossil hominid known as *Sinathropus pekinensis* were discovered in association with animal bones and stone tools. There were also traces of fire. In all the partial remains of about forty-five individuals were discovered, but unfortunately all the material disappeared during the Second World War. It is generally agreed that the earliest examples were about half a million years old, but there was little or no evidence for any significant change in the physical characteristics of the Zhoukoutian population over a long period.

Two further finds, in 1959 and 1966, confirm this impression and also the relationship with fossil hominids from Java, Indonesia. Such a connection is also suggested by a jaw and part of a skull found at two locations at Lantian, Shaanxi, near Xian, similar to the East Javanese *Pithecanthropus robustus*, and somewhat earlier in date than the specimens from the region of Beijing. Older still, perhaps a million years, are jaws of a giant pre-hominid ape *Gigantopithecus* sp. from Guangxi. These toolmaking hominids from Lantian onwards lived before the deposition of the loessic soils which cover much of north-western China. Later remains, from Guangdong, Hubei and Mongolia, show more advanced forms than the Neanderthals of western Eurasia but are still not *Homo sapiens*.

The climate was milder than that of present-day northern China with extensive woodland, open grassland and thick scrub. A small ox, horse, deer, gazelle and hare were grassland fauna; bear, porcupine and boar inhabited the woodlands, while many varieties of rodent characterised the scrub. The presence of rhinoceros points to the existence of pools and marshes, now rare in northern China. It was probably colder than western Europe in Middle Pleistocene times. The carnivores included lion, hyena and panther, while sabre-toothed tiger is attested at Zhoukoutian.

The Upper Cave at Zhoukoutian and other finds from Sichuan and Guangxi provide evidence for the emergence of *Homo sapiens* about 50,000 years ago, at a time when the loess was being formed. The skeletal material indicates that at this time the basic human types now found in eastern Asia were in the process of formation.

Yangshao

At first the winds brought sand into the Huang He valley where it formed deposits up to 330 feet (100 metres) deep. These were later redeposited on the great plains which flank the lower reaches of the Yellow River. It seems likely that the agricultural potential of the loess in the upstream areas was the first to be exploited, and later the richer and marshier regions further downstream. The role of the hunter-gatherer was still substantial: the composite bow, probably developed in Siberia and still the main weapon of that region until the introduction of the hand-gun, was the means of exploiting the grassland fauna.

On the loess farming began to be practised, and potting and weaving, together with the production of polished stone tools, marked the beginning of the neolithic phase, though it is unlikely that the eastern regions were manageable until a much later period. Nor is there evidence for more than hunter-fisher communities in the valley of the Chang Jiang where, even after the introduction of pottery, it was a long while before settlement farming became the normal pattern. It was the specific nature of the loess which contributed to the pattern of development in the Yellow River valley, where settlements seem to have been able to continue without soil exhaustion over very long periods, for the water retained in the loess brings mineral salts to the surface to renew the fertility of the soil.

The first neolithic site investigated was at Yangshao, Henan. This was in 1921 when stone tools and red coil-made pottery decorated in black were discovered. More sites were found in Henan and a research programme was started in Gansu in an attempt to trace links with western Asia. More than fifty sites were located, including

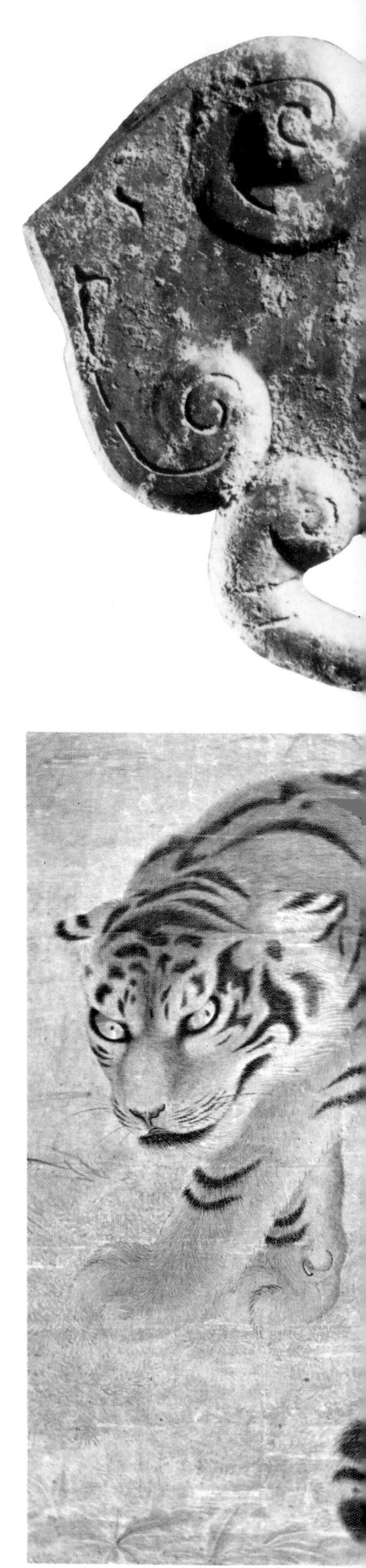

Left. A bronze cheekpiece in the shape of a tiger's head. Hanging from a helmet, it was used to protect the face of the wearer in battle. Shang dynasty. British Museum, London.

Opposite left. Ritual vessel for holding wine, of the type called *hu*. The decoration, of hunting scenes, shows bows and arrows and axes being wielded against buffalo and birds. The mainstay of the early Yellow River peoples, hunting remained important in the historical period. Huai River style, late Zhou or Qin dynasty, sixth to third century B.C. Minneapolis Institute of Arts, Minnesota.

Left below. Tiger leaping down a hill. Tigers were honoured as the emblems of the west, the direction of Kunlun and the Western Paradise; but they were also feared, for if one ate a human his or her soul became the tiger's slave and preyed upon other humans. Painting by Zhen Zhuzhong. British Museum, London.

Below. Bronze pole-end, showing on one side a fierce human face surmounted by a *taotie*, split animal mask, and on the other side a deer and an elephant, creatures which in prehistoric times inhabited northern China. Such a ritual object would be significant both to hunters and to farmers. British Museum, London.

a grave with splendid funerary pottery at Banshan, but more recent work has shown, and C-14 dating has confirmed, that the sites in the central region are earlier than those to the north-west.

What has yet to be found is an earlier neolithic phase than that known at present. It has been suggested that the Yellow River has itself obliterated the evidence, for it is known to have undergone substantial changes of course, the most obvious example being in 1852 when the river mouth shifted from the south to the north of Shandong Peninsula. But while the beginnings of the Chinese neolithic have yet to be found, much has been learned of its mature phases in recent years, the most notable instance being the site of Banpo in a suburb of Xian, Shaanxi.

At Banpo a substantial village was found with successive occupation layers lasting for perhaps two millennia from about 4000 B.C. It had a population of around 300, who first lived in circular wattle and daub huts but later built square or rectangular houses with a planking frame, sunk into the ground to a depth of about 3 feet (1 metre). One building over 40 feet (12 metres) long was set on three rows of posts. The village was divided into three zones: habitation, pottery manufacture and burial. Pigs, dogs and goats were raised; millet was the staple crop. Irrigation was almost certainly practised and a surrounding ditch may have served as a reservoir. There is evidence for group burials which has been taken to point to matriarchy.

There were a number of kilns of two types, one having a cylindrical tunnel providing a forced draught to a beehive-shaped chamber. A firing temperature of about 1000°C was possible. Coarse grey and red wares were found and also a fine, burnished red ware painted in black with geometric designs and, more rarely, human faces or fishes. In one or two cases fish and face seem to have been combined. Various objects such as spindlewhorls were made of clay, but much fine work was done in bone, including fishhooks and arrowheads. Fibre cloth and basketry were also made. Water-deer, sika and bamboo rat seem to have been hunted.

Although it has been suggested that group burials are evidence of a matriarchal society, in fact most of the graves are single. Orientation of the dead is with head to the west or the north-west, the body supine. Three pots were usually placed in the grave. In a few cases the bodies were in coffins. Simple ornaments, stone beads, cut shell, pottery bracelets, were also placed with the dead. The pattern is common to the Yangshao culture to which Banpo belongs.

In the treatment of the dead there is evidence for practices which were to persist into the bronze-using cultures. But neither in the graves, nor elsewhere at Banpo, is there any trace of images or of talismans: only in the pottery decoration is there any evidence for possible symbolic usage. There is no evidence for any temple or shrine in the village, though it is

always possible that the largest building may have been used for ritual purposes as well, perhaps, as serving as the house of the chief. In their trabeation and pounded earth walls the houses set a pattern which is to be found in Korea and Japan until the present day.

Longshan

The next neolithic phase is apparently that first discovered at Chengziyai, Shandong, near Dragon Mountain or Long Shan after which it is named, usually still in the old spelling Lungshan. This culture seems to have originated in Shandong with some outlying sites in the Chang Jiang delta. It is characterised by a fine, thin-walled, black burnished ware made on a fast wheel. Settlements were often on knolls above the surrounding lowlands, which were wetter than the central loesses. Millet, rice and wheat were cultivated, but the settlements were, it seems, smaller than those of Yangshao.

This culture is essentially connected with the eastern coastal zone and does not appear to have reached north-western China. It is generally found overlying Yangshao and immediately preceding layers with Shang material. Some culture traits of the latter can already be detected in the Longshan material. There is some evidence that a phase known at Qijiaping, in Hubei, shows a mixed Yangshao-Lungshan facies between the two.

The superb pottery from Longshan sites has a curiously metallic appearance: certain forms anticipate bronze vessels of the Shang period. The most notable of these is the tripod, *li* or *ding* in later terminology, which consisted of three pointed, ovoid vessels joined at the top, thus providing greater stability and a far larger surface to be heated. A further addition of a circular vessel with a pierced base furnished the prototype for the bronze *xian* or steamer.

Another trait which anticipated Shang practice is the use of bone or shell for predicting the future. Heat was applied to the surface of a prepared blade-bone or piece of tortoise-shell. This produced cracks which were then 'read' as the answer to a question put by the person seeking an oracle. It is also possible that certain shapes in worked stone – a circle, a flat disc and a square ring with a circular hole which later were of great ritual significance – had already some ritual value.

Opposite. Pottery bowl: red ware with black decoration. The stylised face, in a quite other mode from the bronze period *taotie* mask, is found on other examples, also in association with fish, here shown as a schematised rhomboid. In one case, two fish appear to be whispering into the ears of the human head whose headdress may suggest a shamanical role. The marks on the rim are, I believe, to allow the bowl to be orientated. Banpo, Shaanxi. Neolithic period.

Following page. Neolithic vessel from a cemetery site in Gansu. Pottery of this type was the first to lead to the investigation of prehistoric sites in China. The decoration, which was applied by brush using haematite and iron oxide as pigments, was originally believed to have been confined to mortuary vessels, and attempts were made to analyse its significance in terms of such usage. More recently, however, similar pots have been found on habitation sites. Östasiatiska Museet, Stockholm.

Below. A bronze *zun*, ritual vessel for holding wine, in the shape of two rams with a *taotie* mask between them. A variety of animals were domesticated and became familiar motifs as early as the Longshan period. Shang dynasty, twelfth to eleventh century B.C. British Museum, London.

The First Historical Period

Chinese tradition knows nothing of prehistory in the archaeologist's sense, for it maintains that the social and technological developments which are today attributed to the mesolithic and neolithic periods were the work of the San Huang and the Wu Di, the Three Sovereigns and the Five Emperors, to whom it assigns a regnal period of 647 years from 2852 B.C. According to the tradition, these culture heroes were followed by three dynasties, Xia (439 years), Shang whose name was changed to Yin by the Emperor Pangeng (644 years), and Zhou (867 years). Of the historicity of the last there was no doubt, but until the excavations at Anyang, north of Zhengzhou, Henan, which began in 1927, that of Shang-Yin had been doubted. The existence of Xia has yet to be determined, but it is possible that it was contemporaneous with Shang. An alternative suggestion is that it was an invention of Zhou historians who wished to justify the overthrow of Shang on the grounds that its existence was the result of an act of usurpation.

The Shang

Literary sources had spoken of Shang for more than two millennia before archaeological evidence for its existence was obtained. According to the *Shi jing* Book of Odes, Tian (Heaven) gave orders to the black bird (*xuan niao*), which descended and gave birth to Shang. This observation is further expanded in the *Shi ji*, the first history of China written in the first century B.C. by Sima Qian.

Although it had long been known that the last Shang capital was Yinxu, the Wilderness of Yin, its location was not precisely determined but, right at the end of the nineteenth century, thousands of pieces of inscribed bone and tortoise-shell began to be found on the outskirts of Xiaotun, a village near Anyang. These were sold to local apothecaries as dragon-bones, a highly valued drug which was ground up as medicine. A noted scholar who saw some examples recognised the inscriptions as being in an earlier version of the archaic script already known from Zhou ritual bronzes. This had long been the subject of study by literati.

Scholars began to collect the dragon-bones and villagers to search for them with greater enthusiasm, until at last the source for them became known and its significance was realised. The search for the bones led to the discovery of splendid bronzes which dealers sold to collectors in China and abroad. Study of the bones revealed that they were concerned with Great Shang City. Towards the end of the 1920s the controlled exploration of the site began and by 1935 some three hundred graves had been investigated, ten of these of great size and reckoned as royal tombs.

Excavations from 1954 onwards at Zhengzhou, south of the Yellow River, have revealed an earlier capital, while a rich site at Erlitou on the Le River had been suggested as the location of Bo, the capital of Tang, descendant of the black bird and founder of the dynasty. Here there was evidence for a bronze foundry, turquoise, shell and jade ornaments, as well as bronze objects and at least three new pottery forms which were soon to be translated into bronze vessels. Some marks on the ceramics suggest an early script.

A major problem emerges clearly at these sites in Yanshi district: there is no sign of the tentative experiments

in bronze working that characterise the beginnings of the western Eurasian bronze cultures. At the same time the differences in metallurgical techniques are sufficient to rule out direct borrowings from further west, though the idea of bronze working may have been acquired in this way.

At present all the sites investigated show a direct transition from the neolithic to Shang, though earlier sites obviously do not display the sophistication of later ones. At Zhengzhou itself the lower strata show a Longshan facies, but the layers above these, Erligang and Minggonglu, occupy developing phases in Shang culture, the last being equated with the lower phases at Anyang and showing a distinct decline at Zhengzhou. It was originally thought that Shang was centred on the Henan plain, with interests to the north and north-west. There, during the Anyang period, it was already in conflict with Zhou. Evidence has emerged of Shang bronzes and the like in Shandong, while more recently it has become clear that Shang influences extended as far south as Hunan, south of the Yangtze in the kingdom of Chu with which we shall be concerned later.

By the Zhengzhou phase major Shang sites were surrounded by a massive wall of pounded earth, made with small diameter rammers in layers about 1½ inches (4 centimetres) thick. A similar technique was used for the foundations of major ritual buildings at Anyang. There is clear evidence for internal sub-divisions in which both royal and ritual buildings were accompanied by human sacrifices both in the foundations and on adjacent areas. Slaves and prisoners-of-war, both classified with animals on Shang inventories, provided most of the victims, but not all can have belonged to these classes.

The basic features which distinguish the Shang culture from that of earlier periods are the use of bronze, the development of writing and the possession of the chariot. We have already noted the sophistication of the metalworking which seems, incidentally, to have relied on the extensive use of piece moulds rather than the *cire-perdue* method, however complicated the casting. A number of the bronze vessels found on early Shang sites are translations into metal of Longshan forms, another instance of cultural continuity at this time, while new Shang ceramic shapes were rapidly produced in metal also. We may note in passing that Shang potters copied metal vessels in a smooth grey ware. They also used pure kaolin with a carved and stamped decoration: this repeats motifs found on bronzes on white vessels of great elegance, and a true felspathic glaze. This points to high kiln temperatures (up to 1200°C), a fact which suggests a high degree of furnace control, important also in metal-working.

The elements of writing hinted at in the Longshan period were rapidly developed to provide some 5000 characters by the Anyang phase, characters of which perhaps half are recognisable as prototypes for those still in use. Comparisons with the beginnings of writing in ancient Sumer and Egypt show that the process seems to have been very similar where and whenever bronze came into use. A need to record and list led to the use of simplified drawings of objects being used as 'catchwords' in ledgers: requirements for greater precision involved the introduction of means of qualifying the original simplicities. The Shang scribes soon turned their skills to writing complex sentences posing questions of state to the gods and ancestors, on the dragon-bones.

The Shang chariot does not, at present, seem to have any forerunner in east Asia and its general features are similar to those of Eurasiatic types. In two respects, however, the Chinese model is distinguished. The wheels had many fine spokes, unlike chariots found further west, and the method of harnessing the two horses which involved a yoke was both different and more efficient. The vehicles seem to have been introduced at the time of the move to Anyang and are thus comparable in date with the earliest examples found in the Middle East. The composite bow, now with bronze-tipped arrows, survived from the neolithic period, together with the *go*, the dagger-axe, in a bronze form (though this also occurs in jade, often elaborately hafted, clearly a ritual weapon) and the *chi* axe with a flared blade like that of the headsman. These, when in bronze, are often decorated on the blade: a splendid example from a grave at Yidu, Shandong, has an *à-jour* mask of a face flanked by vignettes of a libation scene beside the mouth.

Shang Beliefs

All the elements which we have discussed, bronze, writing and sophisticated weapons, including the chariot, were linked to a very great extent to the royal and aristocratic sections of the Shang state and with their preoccupations with rituals and oracles, dependent upon their relationship with their ancestors, both immediate and more remote. The latter seem not to have a genealogical or chronological order but were figures, with personal names, from the remote past. But they, and the more recently dead, were the subject of endless offerings and questions, by means of the oracle bones which were themselves used to ascertain the appropriate offering in each instance.

It was not possible, generally speaking, to address the supreme being, Shang Di, directly, but the system was dependent on what has been called 'optimistic rationalism' and 'a faith that if the appropriate offering can be made to the correct ancestor on the proper day, all will be well for the Shang' (Allan). Two further considerations seem to have obtained: the ancestors had to be available; available ancestors had to be in a good mood.

The idea that each individual has two souls, the *hun* and *po*, may already have existed, or developed during the Shang period. Of these, the first could in principle make its way to heaven, though what happened to it there is not very clear. The *po* on the other hand stayed in the vicinity of the body and could, if well-treated by the living, provide a link with the world of Shang Di and lesser deities. The journey that faced the *hun* was extremely hazardous and it seems likely that some effort was made to persuade it not to risk it. A *po*, and presumably a *hun*, that stayed near the living would, if not satisfied with its posthumous treatment, prove dangerous and maleficent. An extravagant scheme of offerings and funerary rites was instituted to avoid such a calamity; such a scheme increased in its magnificent extravagance with the relative importance of the dead to be

Opposite. A *taotie* of the Shang or Yin period. This horned dragon or tiger monster lost its body as a punishment for eating human beings and was known as 'the glutton'. Its head or mask appears repeatedly in various stylised forms in the early artefacts. The eyebrows are *gui* dragons. Östasiatiska Museet, Stockholm.

Below. A *guang*, or vessel in which ceremonial millet wine was mixed, showing the fine detail achieved in bronze metallurgy by the Shang. The decorative motifs of the vessel itself are *taotie* masks, while the lid is modelled as a tiger's or dragon's head with a serpent's tail curling behind. The handle consists of another mythical animal. Minneapolis Institute of Arts, Minnesota.

honoured. Evidence from such activities, together with the inscriptions on oracle bones, furnish us with some understanding of the Shang view of the world and the powers which, in some way, control it.

Burials of members of the royal family and of the nobility provide the most striking examples of the manner in which the powerful dead were treated. Attempts were made to preserve the body; unsuccessfully, for the Shang lacked the techniques of mummification known in contemporary Egypt.

The interment took place in a shaft grave, some 9-11 yards (8-10 metres) deep with slightly sloping walls, which led to a timber burial chamber. Beneath this were pits which contained sacrifices, both animal and human, some of whom seem to have been buried alive. These victims were separated from the burial chamber by a layer of charcoal. At the bottom of the rectangular shaft was a step on which bodies in wooden coffins were found (although there was none in the burial chamber of the Yidu, Shandong, tomb on which this account is based; it had been robbed in antiquity). From the step, ramps led to the surface: these were cardinally orientated, that on the south being the true entrance. (This may be connected with a later belief that north was the direction of death.)

The entrance to the tomb itself held three layers of human offerings, killed *in situ*: there were twenty-four skulls and thirteen skeletons, all young males. Two great bronze axes found on the step were probably the sacrificial weapons. Despite looting in antiquity, objects placed in the chamber can be determined to some extent. They included bronze ritual vessels, jade objects, cowries (used as money), spearheads and arrowheads. The whole shaft and the approaches were sealed by thin, rammed layers of sand and loam arranged alternately. From other sites it is clear that the body in the tomb was richly attired and accompanied by jewels and jade, the latter of ritual intention.

The bronze vessels, too, were classified according to function: preparation and presentation of food, both grain and meat; holding millet wine; drinking wine; holding ablution water; pouring ablution water. As Watson has pointed out the various vessels came in a variety of forms for most of the categories, and laid the foundations for the elaborate *batterie d'offrandes*, if one may so put it, which so delighted Song antiquarians two and a half millennia later. Other objects were also buried: an apparent animal lover had an elephant and

Left. Bronze *ding* from Ningxiang, Hunan, bearing the inscription *da he*, great grain. This may refer to the substance that it would have held on ritual occasions. On the other hand, similar vessels decorated with animal heads seem to have indicated the particular flesh, of deer, bull, dog etc., which they contained as a sacrificial offering. Watson thinks the human face represents an enemy who was offered as a sacrifice. Late Shang.

Below. A bronze *qi*, ceremonial axe, of the Shang period. Axes of this type, which had stone prototypes, were used for the decapitation of victims at the great ritual burials and were sometimes left beside the bodies. They often include an inscription in a cartouche *ya-xing* in the

various other beasts interred in the vicinity of his tomb.

The most striking examples of objects buried in the tomb, however, are the battle-chariots, complete with horses and driver, occasionally accompanied by a second man. These have been recovered at Anyang and elsewhere in the form of negative moulds which have preserved the shapes in the loessic soils. It seems that the charioteer and the horses were killed first and placed in the grave, distinct from the main burial, and that the chariot was then placed in position. Pits adjacent to the principal tomb were sometimes used to accommodate other offerings.

At Wuguancun, Anyang, fifty human skulls were found, in addition to the skeletons of twenty-four women and twenty-two men on the step and both ramps as well as in the burial chamber itself. This seems to have been furnished with an intricate canopy of painted leather, bamboo and bark. Some of the victims at Wuguancun seem to have died peacefully, but the majority were slain.

The practice of killing people to accompany the dead was generally abandoned after the Shang dynasty, though chariot burials persisted for some centuries after the accession of Zhou. However, the pattern for noble burials was set and was to persist thereafter, the human servitors and slaves being replaced by wooden or ceramic models which might be present in some hundreds or even thousands. It is reported that Shi Huang Di's great tomb included the bodies of his wives and the workmen who built the enormous structure. This was an underground palace with grounds which symbolised the empire and the ocean, according to Sima Qian who wrote about a hundred years after the death of Emperor Shi Huang Di in 210 B.C.

Such then were the material benefits provided for the powerful and recent dead, who seem to have been thought of as at once near Shang Di, present in the tomb, and in the Yellow Springs, a kind of underground limbo which Granet called 'the true dwelling place of the dead'. But there had also to be a continuing cult of the dead, with offerings of an appropriate nature on the correct occasions: it is with such matters that the oracle bones are concerned.

Offerings were made to (Shang) Di, the Ruler of the Four Quarters, the Eastern and the Western Mothers, the directions East, West and South (but not North), and to various *genii loci*. The sun was also the subject of oracular enquiries, in a formulation which was the same as that used for ancestors. But the word *ri* ('sun') was

space immediately under the ears. This, which seems to imitate a seal impression, may have referred to the clan name. An example from Yidu, Shandong, shows a man pouring a wine offering onto an altar. Museum für Volkerkunde, Berlin.

Right. The animal depicted on this Shang ritual wine vessel is probably a tiger. Its body is decorated with dragons, that of the clinging man with serpents. It is thought that such an image is intended as that of a tutelary spirit. The motif is a circum-Pacific one, occurring among west coast American Indian groups and has close parallels with the *makara* with a figure of a man in its mouth which is found in the Indian sub-continent and in South East Asia. Musée Cernuschi, Paris.

also a word for 'day' in the ten-day week, a matter which becomes important in consideration of the myth of the ten suns (see page 61). The question might be asked, as usual in yes-no terms (oracles using the 0-1 conventions of computers), 'Crack-making on *yizi* day: The king will entertain the sun (*bin ri*); the king will not entertain the sun.'

Initially the king seems to have arrived at correct procedures by a process of trial and error: by the end of the Shang dynasty the rituals had become formulaic and the oracular pronouncement verified what was already prescribed by long practice. At first it had been necessary to determine the day, particular ritual, animal, number, colour and sex, singly or in combinations which might include human offerings: all had to be established by question and answer. By the end, the oracle was something more like a statement in the royal programme. Watson quotes an example from the 1971 excavations at Anyang:

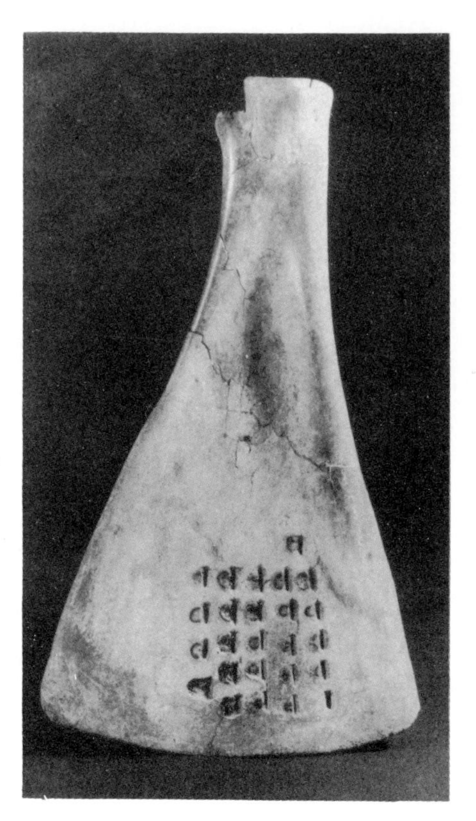

Above. Shang oracle bone with incised questions, formulaic in structure, regarding animal offerings to the ancestors, from Anyang, Henan. Each question was put to the oracle separately by applying a heated bronze point to a prepared pit in the bone. The cracks on the reverse side of the scapula were read as answers and, if the oracle agreed, then the suggested sacrifices were made. Here seven offerings of pigs and one of a dog in a *ding* were proposed.

Left. Two tomb guards from a grave at Jinan in the Huai valley, Henan. While human sacrifices were carried out to provide the Shang ruler at Xiaotun with guards and servants, lesser burials and those of later times were more likely to be provided with such figurines. Národní Galerie, Prague.

Opposite left. The Red Bird or phoenix, which symbolised the south, a cardinal direction honoured by the Shang. The phoenix later became identified with the pheasant, but this bird, with its curved beak and long claws, is of the archaic type: a bird of prey more aptly associated with the arid south. Bas relief from the tomb of Shen in Sichuan. Han dynasty.

Opposite right. Dragon pendant in brown jade. The dragon symbolised the east, one of the deities to which the Shang made sacrifices. Jade ornaments were particularly prized, partly for their intrinsic beauty and partly because it was so difficult to work the hard material with the primitive tools of the Shang. This pendant dates from the later feudal period or Eastern Zhou dynasty (770–256 B.C.). Seattle Art Museum, Washington. Eugene Fuller Memorial Collection.

Get ready the officers. Father Second a pig; son a pig; Mother Ninth a pig. Get ready the overseers. Third in a ting *a dog. Fourth a pig. Ancestor Seventh a pig. Father Second a pig, son a pig.*

Each offering was separately confirmed, though it is not clear whether the questions were put at the moment of offering or in advance. Other more general questions were also put, covering events to come over a specific period or in specific circumstances, or to find out whether Shang Di or the ancestors, presumably by intervention with Di, would produce a good harvest, a successful hunt, or suitable weather: 'It will rain; it will not rain.' With so much at stake, the goodwill of the influential dead was worth the vast expenditure to which the Shang tombs bear witness.

It is interesting to note that after Zhou had overthrown Shang, Wu, the first Zhou ruler, gave the Shang lineage a fief in Song state, where the altar of the god of the soil was at Sang Lin, Mulberry Grove. This was an ancestral shrine for the Shang because it was there that the first ruler Cheng Tang had made an offering of himself. Therefore his descendants needed access to it to remain in touch with their ancestors. The story is first found in texts of the fifth century B.C.

After Tang had defeated Xia and set up the new dynasty there was a great drought which lasted for five, some say seven, years. A black ox was offered at Sang Lin, according to one account, but in a compilation of the third century A.D. we are told that the scribe cracked a bone for Tang and said that it was proper to pray using human offerings. Tang, saying *yu yi ren* 'I the one man' (a phrase, as Allan notes, used in the oracle bones by Shang kings), with cut hair and pared nails, mounted on an unornamented chariot, drawn by white horses, with unfurled banner and wearing a necklace of white dog's tooth couchgrass, offered himself as a victim to Shang Di at Sang Lin. The people rejoiced and the rains fell abundantly.

It is from such beginnings that the theory of the 'Mandate of Heaven' was to be developed in the Zhou period. Xia had been defeated, because the period of that dynasty had come to an end, but Cheng Tang had been responsible for the fall of a ruler who mediated between the people and Shang Di. Such an act, against the order of things, led to drought which could only be ended by the offering of the one responsible. Some credence is lent to this interpretation by the story that after the defeat of Shang by Zhou, Wu the victor and founder of the new dynasty fell ill and the regent Zhou Gong 'prayed in his stead, asking that the sins of the dynasty be visited on himself'.

The Rise of Feudalism and the Unification of China

The Rise of Zhou

The Shang capital finally fell to the troops of Zhou somewhere between 1122 and 1027 B.C., when the last Shang ruler committed suicide. Zhou was one of the peripheral states in an uncertain relationship with Shang, situated in the Weishui valley, Shaanxi. It had steadily grown in power, a fact which the questions in the oracle bones make clear. There is, as well, some evidence to suggest that Shang tried to organise attacks upon Zhou by third parties. At the fall of Anyang, Zhou seems to have already occupied about two-thirds of Shang. It does not, however, appear to have differed culturally from Shang to any marked degree at this time. Sites which have been investigated from the early period show a sequence Yangshao-Longshan-Zhou, and it was not until three centuries or so later, when the capital had been moved to Luoyang, that major changes took place.

Wu, the first Zhou ruler, died shortly after his victory and the first stages in the establishment of the new dynasty were carried out by Zhou Gong, acting as regent during the minority of Wu's son Cheng Wang. He organised the realm into a series of feudal states, including a fief for Shang at Song. Court rituals and the worship of ancestors were further refined to act as a means of strengthening the relationship between the feudatories. At the centre, the emperor performed rites for the state as a whole, while the lords of the constituent elements performed them on behalf of their own followers.

There was a gradual shift from Shang Di to Tian, Heaven, as the central figure in worship. The concept of the Mandate of Heaven became more

complex, as did the idea of *de*, virtue or moral excellence; both these were to play a central role in the teachings of Confucius. At court a *bin-xiang* (Master of Ceremonies) was responsible for the production of complex functions in which art, literature and music were combined to symbolise the state. There were proclamations of imperial orders; these orders, at first written on bamboo slips, were, by the middle of the tenth century, cast in bronze; audiences were held at dawn and dusk, a practice that was to continue for more than three thousand years. Similarly, imperial donations to fief-holders or awards by such lords to their subordinates were recorded on bronze ritual vessels, which were used at the formal ceremonies confirming such acts of patronage.

Such inscriptions are not only valuable documents for the historian but, with such works as the *Shi jing* and the *Shu jing*, the Book of Songs and the Book of Documents, testify, as Sullivan remarks, to 'that sense of history which is one of the most striking features of Chinese civilisation, and, as a corollary, to the almost sacred place held in Chinese life by the written word.' Paradoxically, it was this sense of the importance of the written word which led to its deliberate destruction when Shi Huang Di ordered the burning of books (see page 41).

Under the Zhou, cities grew in size and in wealth. According to the *Kaogong ji* (the Book of Works) which forms part of the *Zhou Li* (Ritual of Zhou), probably compiled under the Western Han but reflecting what was believed to have been ideal dynastic behaviour, a city should consist of a square with sides of nine *li* (about 3 miles or 5 kilometres), each with three gates. The temple to the ancestors should be on the left (east),

Right. A *guei*, ritual food vessel, in bronze from the Zhou period. Such vessels often carry an inscription indicating for which august ancestor's service it was intended and enjoining its preservation in the temple from generation to generation. The name of the ancestor was given in the form of the number of the day in the ten-day week on which the offering was to be made: e.g. Father Six.

Right. An early Zhou *yu* or wine-bucket. This type seems to have occurred at the end of the Shang dynasty and the beginning of Zhou. Such vessels were intended for sacral purposes and may bear inscriptions indicating the name of the maker, the dedicatee, an ancestor, the day of the ten-day week on which offerings were made, and the name of the vessel offered. In this case there is a single character only, which may designate the dedicator. Victoria and Albert Museum, London.

Opposite. Hou Ji, a miraculously born descendant of Huang Di. As one of the gods of the earth, he was made Ruler of the Millet by Tang, founder of the Shang dynasty. When the Shang were supplanted by the Zhou, Hou Ji was called ancestor of the Zhou. Statuette in bronze. Musée Guimet, Paris.

the Altar of the Soil to the right (west). The court where the ruler gave audience was at the front (south), the market at the rear (north). Nine roads, each nine chariot tracks wide, should link the nine gates, parallel to the cardinal axes and forming a chequerboard pattern.

The investigation of cities on the ground is still in its infancy, but their size is certainly impressive, if not quite on the scale envisaged in the *Zhou Li*. A site at Linzixian, Shandong, was 2½ miles square (6.5 square kilometres), with a rammed-earth wall over 10 yards (9 metres) high, though it is interesting to note that the north-south axis was well over twice the east-west and the palace was located in the south-west corner. A similar site in Hebei was considerably larger. Both these cities were the capitals of Zhou feudatories.

Three capitals of Zhou itself are also known: Fengyi, west of Xian, and Hao, slightly closer to the modern city, Luoyang, which was capital for the whole of the Western Zhou period. The Eastern Zhou capital, Wangcheng, was found in the western suburbs of Luoyang. Within the walls the buildings were on high plinths. The wide-eaved, tiled roofs were set on complex timber pillars and bearers; the walls were of rammed earth and the floors were all covered with matting. The largest structures seem to have been ritual centres, while others were palaces and dwellings. Some impression of such buildings, set in successive courtyards, can be found in Arthur Waley's translation of verses from the *Book of Songs*. Sumptuary laws governed the size and style of such buildings, and indicated categorically those plans, designs and patterns which were the prerogative of royalty.

The practice of chariot burials continued well into Zhou times, but large-scale human sacrifices seem to have ceased, though the evidence from major tombs shows that some followers appear to have accompanied the dead. The oracle bones were no longer consulted. Bronze styles altered, though the techniques

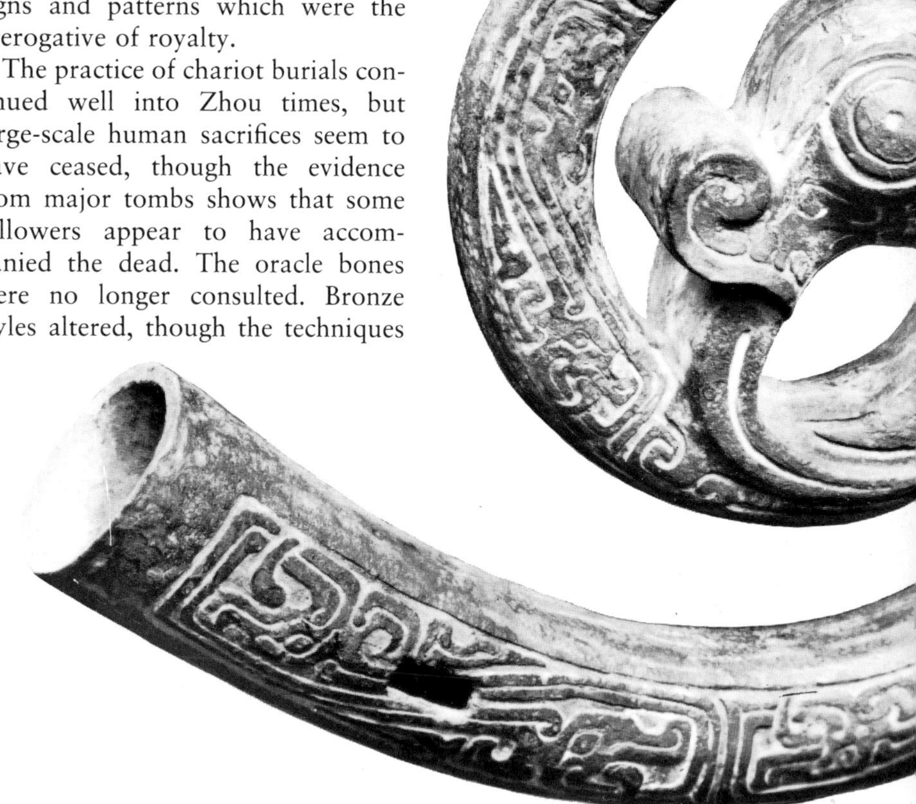

of manufacture remained the same until the fifth century B.C., and probably a hundred years later in the conservative northern areas, when the *cire-perdue* process was introduced. The Shang *taotie* motif was no longer used, but a Zhou innovation appears to have been the introduction of tuned bronze bell chimes among the *mingchi*.

Such bells had been made in the Zhou homeland from the tenth century B.C. Their use in burials may have been to replace the slaughtered musicians. A set of nine is known

Above. Ceremonial jade sceptre used by the king in his all-important mediating role between the state and heaven, Tian. As the king alone was capable of performing the ritual for the benefit of society, it is appropriate that the sceptre combines the circular *bi* symbol of heaven and the axe symbol of royal power. Shang dynasty. Národní Galerie, Prague.

Left. The royal party surveying the site in 770 B.C. for the new Eastern Zhou capital at Luoyang as described in the *Book of Documents*. Once the location had been approved by the tortoise-shell oracle, the king and his uncle surveyed the site and planned its layout in accordance with the principles of geomancy. On the third day after that the work began. The use of the compass is several centuries too early, but the illustration was made more than two and a half millennia after the event. The plate is from the Qing imperial edition of the *Shu jing. Qing-ting Shu jing tusho* published in A.D. 1905.

Centre. Pole end in the form of a horned dragon. The use of mythological symbols to adorn domestic articles and chariot trappings followed an elaborate code established in Shang times. Bronze, Middle Zhou dynasty (900–600 B.C.). William Rockhill Nelson Gallery, Kansas City, Missouri. Nelson Fund.

Opposite above. Bronze tiger with a hollow chamber in the centre. Though the decorative motifs show the Zhou development of Shang culture, the general style is quite different: more massive and in keeping with the power of the dynasty, which came from the west, the direction of the tiger. Zhou dynasty, *c.* tenth century B.C. Freer Gallery of Art, Washington, D.C.

from a tomb of a marquis of Cai at Shouxian, Anhui; another of thirteen from a tomb at Xinyang, Henan, and another nine from a farm near Jucheng, Shandong. The bells are clapperless and are played by being struck on the outside on the panels of nipples which are separated by inscriptions. The sets discovered so far are tuned to recognisable scales and seem to date from the fifth century B.C., the period of Confucius. His works testify to the ritual importance of music and dance. He seems to have been particularly susceptible to music: a famous passage in the *Analects* tells us:

When the Master was in Qi he heard the shao *and for three months did not know the taste of meat.*

The *shao* was music associated with the Emperor Shun: the passage seems to imply that the sage was so moved that he did not notice what he was eating. But he was dogmatic on the propriety of the various forms of music. Bells and stone chimes furnished the great ceremonial music *jia yue*: it was improper to employ this at ceremonies outside the city. This was the music of the rulers. The lute and the flute were appropriate for nobility and officers of state, while the people made music with earthenware drums. Such ritual music was generally accompanied by dances prescribed for the occasion.

According to the Han scholar Xu Shen jade possesses five virtues: charity, rectitude, wisdom, courage and equity. These are exemplified by its bright, warm lustre; its translucency; the purity and penetration of its note when struck; its capacity to break but not bend; its sharp angles which do no harm.

As we have noted it seems already to have been valued in neolithic times, while for the Shang, especially in the Anyang period, the skill and versatility of the lapidaries reached almost incredible heights. Most of their work was on thin slabs, though a few pieces in the round have been discovered: knives and *go*, ornaments for clothing in the shapes of birds and animals, beads and handles for knives. Wisdom was superbly represented by a slab just under a yard (0.8 metres) long, decorated on one side with the design of a tiger from a late Shang grave at Wuguancun. There were also various ritual objects: discs *bi*, rings and *zong*, which comprised a square-section tube surrounding a circular one that acted as a shield for the ancestor tablet. The latter was conceived as a phallus and came to symbolise earth.

As might be expected the use of ritual jades increased in Zhou times, especially in the Eastern Zhou period, while the *Zhou Li* gives detailed instructions for the use of jade for the living as well as for the dead. At audiences the king, the princes and the various ranks of the nobility held jade objects of different shapes. Other pieces were used to signify royal authority: messengers carried a *yazhong*

Left. Bell of the Huai style (late Zhou), decorated with dragon and *taotie* motifs. Such bronze bells, oval in cross section, were used not only in the performance of music at court (which Confucians thought conducive to morality), but also played an important part in the rituals of the *wu* shamans. The bells thus acquired the supernatural qualities illustrated in the myth of the dog and the princess. Minneapolis Institute of Arts, Minnesota. Bequest of Alfred F. Pillsburg, 1950.

Opposite. This selection of jade objects, ranging in date from the eleventh century B.C. to the seventeenth century A.D., shows how the art of the jade-carver has continued to serve both ritual and decorative ends. British Museum, London.

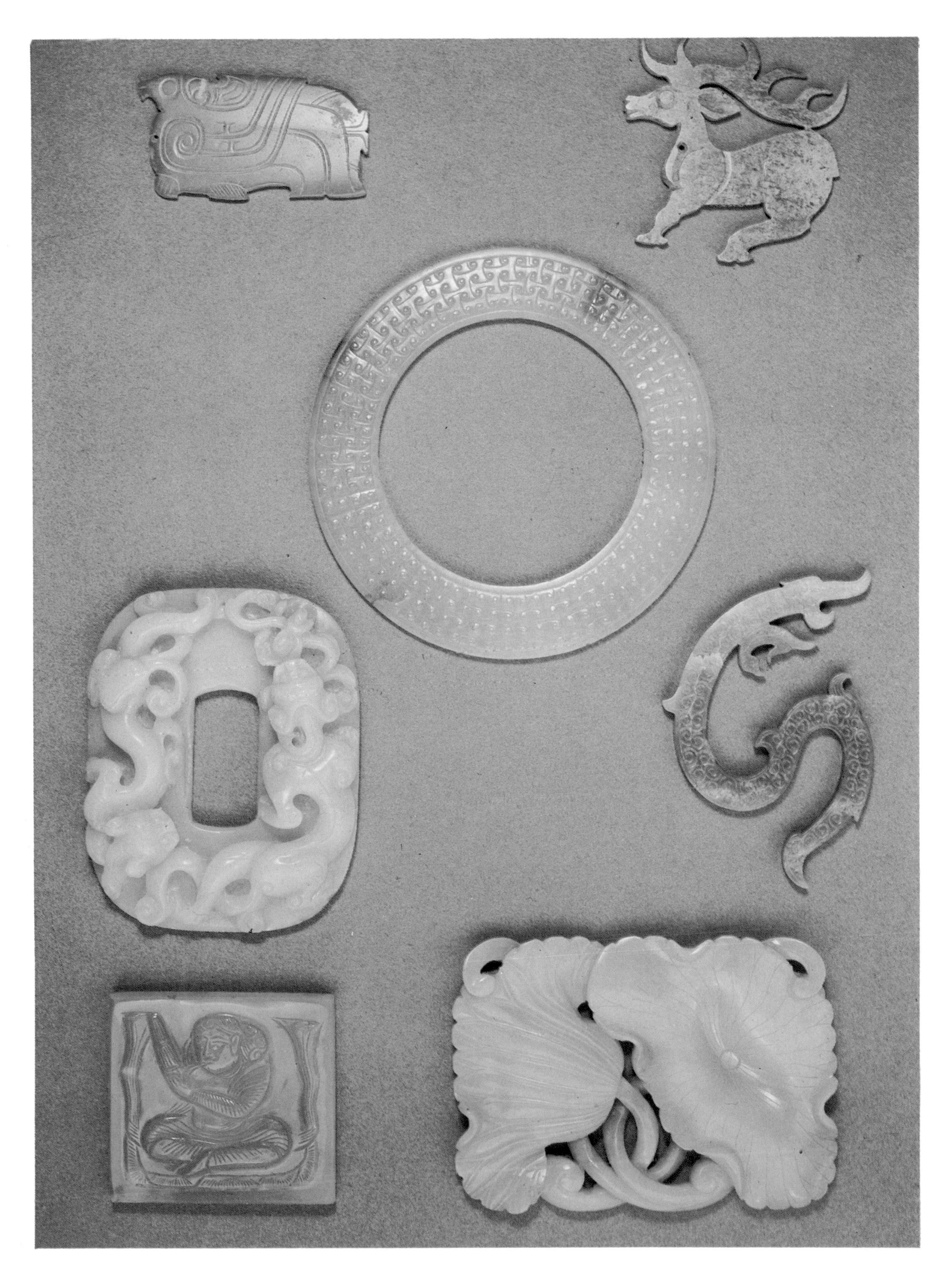

(jade knife) with a mobilisation order, envoys were protected by a piece with a concave butt, *yenguei*. The powerful dead were accompanied in the grave by pieces of jade ritually disposed about the supine body: *bi* on the chest, *zong* under the back, symbols of heaven and earth, a semi-circular *huang* at the feet, north, a *zhang* at the head, south, a sceptre *guei* to the east and a tiger to the west. Plugs of jade sealed the seven orifices of the body and a cicada-shaped piece was laid on the tongue. All these were designed to preserve the body as a home for the soul or souls, but the final extravagance is to be found in the famous jade suits of thin jade plaques stitched with gold thread, which encased the bodies of Prince Liu Sheng and his wife Dou Wan, who died at the end of the second century B.C. and were buried at Mancheng, Hebei. Nothing of their bodies survived.

Qin Shi Huang Di

As time passed the power of Zhou to control its feudatories steadily diminished and the period of the Warring States (480-221 B.C.) is aptly named. Most of central China and that to the north and south of the Yangtze (Chang Jiang) estuary came under the control of Chu, a state which had marked connections with the south, long recognised as a centre of artistic achievement. Meanwhile, to the west of Xian, Qin was increasing in power and territorial extent. By 256 what remained of Zhou had been annexed and in 223 Qin overthrew Chu, though Chu's importance as a cultural centre was considerable during the Han period. By 221 B.C. all China (which did not then include all the territory between the Yangtze and the present southern frontier) was united under a single ruler, Qin Shi Huang Di for the first time.

During this troubled period further changes in the style and decoration of bronze vessels took place: these included the return of the *taotie*. Animal motifs similar to those of the Central Asian steppe cultures appeared but it seems likely that the similarities are the result of Chinese influence upon the art of the nomads rather than the other way round as western scholars used to think. Excavations in and around Huixian, south-west of Anyang, once in the ancient state of Wei, revealed a curious reversion to Shang practice: nineteen chariots were buried, their horses being interred separately. Other graves produced bronzes with gold and silver inlay, and a richness of jades. Around Luoyang several hundred graves have been investigated which reveal very large numbers of ritual vessels. Splendid bronze mirrors were another feature of the Luoyang burials.

There is evidence for the emergence of a wealthy, non-noble class: its members employing craftsmen to

Right. It was long believed that the animal art of Central Asia, as for example in the pieces from the Ordos, originated there, perhaps partly under influences from further west. Recent discoveries in China suggest that the peoples of Central Asia borrowed many of the original motifs from Chinese sources. They seemed to have retained a preference for stylised, almost two-dimensional forms in low relief. Some of these are to be seen in the bronze repertory of Dian.

Opposite. Two warriors. The Zhou dynasty gradually crumbled during the period known as the Warring States, from 480 to 221 B.C. The art of war and of the deployment of armies was markedly developed during the long struggle. The symbolism of power was never far from mind, as the traditional accoutrement of these warriors shows. Daoist scroll painting. Religionskundliche Sammlung der Universität, Marburg.

furnish their daughters with gilded bronzes as part of their dowries and adorning their own furnishings and carriages with bronze fittings inlaid with precious metals and malachite. Such manifestations of wealth could no doubt be justified by the same arguments which Sullivan has quoted from the *Guanzi*:

Lengthen the period of mourning so as to occupy people's time, and elaborate the funeral so as to spend their money. . . . To have large pits for burial is to provide work for poor people; to have magnificent tombs is to provide work for artisans. To have inner and outer coffins is to encourage carpenters, and to have many pieces for the enshrouding is to encourage seamstresses.

It is hard to imagine what a Shang or a Zhou Master of Ceremonies would have made of such a passage.

Meanwhile various developments were taking place on the Chinese marches. Horse-riding nomads, armed with the composite bow, were forcing the Chinese to replace their battle chariots with cavalry. Secondly the development of the forged long-sword in iron, some two centuries after the first production of iron objects about 500 B.C., provided a formidable weapon for the great armies of foot soldiers who transformed military tactics towards the close of the Warring States period. Against the nomadic raiders the Chinese built walls, which were finally linked up under Shi Huang Di to form the Great Wall.

To the south-west an interesting development took place in Yunnan. A force from Chu had made its way there in the third century B.C. and, its line of retreat cut by Qin armies moving southwards, it settled there and established a kingdom known as Dian. In 108 B.C. the Han dynasty, Qin's successor, imposed suzerainty on Dian. In the 80s they completed a process of expansion southwards which had begun on the Yellow River two millennia or so earlier. Excavations at Shizhaishan, near Kunming, revealed a royal cemetery which yielded objects of Chinese origin, others with clear affinities with Ordos and the steppe, others again closely linked with bronze material from the Dongson culture of Vietnam and, finally and most important, pieces which depict ritual and other scenes in three-dimensional figures set on a platform, or fights between cavalrymen and foot soldiers. These appear to be without parallel. Cattle, birds and snakes seem to have had cultural significance.

It was, allegedly, the southward campaigns of Qin which led to the foundation of Dian, campaigns which culminated in the first unification of China under Shi Huang Di, the ruler who arrogated to himself the title of First Emperor. His armies fought in the extreme south, in Korea and against the Xiongnu on the line of the Great Wall. He built roads, and controlled weights and measures. 'Where doubt existed he established a clear single standard.' He tried to curtail the growing power of the merchant class. He built great palaces, linked by walled roads so that none might know where he was lodged, and created for his tomb a vast mound some 47 yards (43 metres) high, set in a double enclosure whose outer walls were 2396 by 1065 yards (2173 by 974 metres).

It was looted soon after his death and has yet to be excavated, but preliminary investigations suggest the presence of thousands of life-sized figures. Sima Qian reports that the tomb at Xian covered an underground palace and a model of the empire, with its rivers and seas filled with mercury. Those of the royal women who had not borne children were killed to accompany their royal master in the next world, while all those who worked on the site were trapped by secret machinery within the walls. Confucius is said to have warned that the making of clay and wooden figures was a dangerous practice since it might lead to the reversion to deplorable ancient acts. Shi Huang Di, who on the advice of his minister Li Si in 213 B.C. burnt the books which did not deal with divination, agriculture, arboriculture and medicine, proved him right.

The Han Consolidation

Qin Shi Huang Di's victory over Chu brought about the first unification of China. The emperor died in 210 B.C. and was succeeded by his son whose assassination three years later marked the beginning of a rebellion by a former bandit Liu Bang and the Chu general Xiang You. After the fall of the Qin capital the general proclaimed himself king of Chu while Liu Bang made himself king of Han, a former feudal state to the north of Chu. A war broke out between the two states which after four years ended in the suicide of Xiang You.

Liu Bang was proclaimed Emperor of Han, took the name Gaozu and established his capital at Changan. The dynasty thus initiated was to last until A.D. 221, with a brief interregnum, Xin, A.D. 9-23: the period before Xin is referred to as Western or Former Han, that after as Eastern or Later. Much of the energy of the early Han rulers was devoted to battles or negotiations with the Xiongnu, whose activities in northern China had been greatly stimulated by the fall of Qin and their own successes against their rivals, the Western Turks or Yuezhi.

It was as a result of these campaigns that China first appears to have become aware of the world to its west when the Emperor Wu (140-87 B.C.) sent his general Zhang Qian into Central Asia in 138 B.C. on an abortive mission to arrange an alliance with the Yuezhi against their mutual enemy. The mission, which lasted twelve years, failed in its first objective, but its consequences were very considerable.

Zhang's discovery that Chinese bamboo and silk had reached Central Asia by way of India indicated to him that there was a southerly route

westwards from China which did not pass through territory subject to threats of disruption from the Xiongnu. This in its turn led to Han expansion southwards, ultimately as far as the region of Hue, Vietnam, as well as into Yunnan to annex Dian, in a search for ports and land routes on the way to India, the ports of the Persian Gulf and finally to Rome.

This last became known to China during the Han period as a great power in the far west, and as another potential ally against the nomads who disrupted the Eurasian trade. Rome (or more accurately the eastern parts of the Roman empire) was given the name Da Qin, Great Qin after Shi Huang Di's first empire, a name which led to that by which Zhongguo, the Middle Kingdom, is known in most western languages: China.

That very little by way of direct contacts came of these first intelligences was due not only to the vast distances involved and the fact that the Chinese proper were not a seagoing people. It was also due to the vested interests of all those intermediaries along the routes who recognised a threat to their trade by which Chinese silks, lacquers and ceramics were to reach the west and exotic fruits from the Middle East and the great horses from Ferghana, so much larger and more powerful than those native to the area, reached China.

This enlargement of Chinese ideas of the world also had a profound importance in the growth of Chinese ideas about the world of the spirits. As Watson has put it: '. . . the intellectual release effected by the removal of Shi Huang Di's oppression of theoretical discussion and writing led to a burst of creative scholarship. Texts were edited and historical documents scanned in an effort to reach an objective assessment of tradition in all its aspects. On the one hand Confucian philosophy was gradually rescued from its recent retreat and began to infiltrate the ranks of the official class. On the other, attention to popular superstitions and mythology became respectable among the educated.'

Among the themes that emerged was that of Xi Wang Mu, Queen Mother of the West, who lived somewhere in the vicinity of Mount Kunlun which was also an *axis mundi*. Xi Mu, Mother of the West, had been one of the recipients of offerings in Shang times, but little is known of her or whether she was in fact the prototype for Xi Wang Mu. The latter was, in later times, a source of the elixir of immortality and indeed gave this to Yi the archer (see page 65), from whom his wife stole it before she fled to the moon. The moon is also linked with the west, in contrast to the sun which is always associated with the east. And in the east there is another source of immortality, Penglai, the island of the immortals. It is said that Qin Shi Huang Di, advised by Daoists at his court, sent a party of noble boys and girls across the ocean to seek for the island, but they never returned. Dong Wang Gong was the male equivalent of Xi Wang Mu in the east: they used to meet from time to time (see page 80).

Such beliefs entered into Chinese records during Han times, though it is likely that there were already elements of them in the texts destroyed under the Qin dynasty. To what extent Han reconstructions modified the earlier versions in the interests of neo-Confucian orthodoxy is a matter for debate. But in Han art we can see evidence for a growing interest in mythological and legendary themes. Recent archaeological work has greatly enlarged the range of data.

In the early stages of the Han dynasty the work of artists and of craftsmen reflected the conservative traditions of officials and scholars who were engaged in the restoration of the *status quo*, the styles and manners of the Warring States. At the

Left above. The carriage of an Eastern Han official represented as a tomb model in bronze. The driver is shown behind a wide dashboard, another servant probably held a leading rein. The harness, which was developed during the second century A.D., was extremely efficient. The umbrella is a symbol of authority, as is the axe which is found on other models in the Wuwei tombs.

Left. Bronze horses from Wuwei, Gansu. These models, like very many others from the same location, depict 'celestial horses', the acquisition of which from their breeders in Ferghana and Sogdiana had followed on Zhang Qian's mission to the Far West under the Western Han emperor Wudi. These famous 'blood-sweating' beasts became symbols of prestige: in Eastern Han times, when the Wuwei examples were cast, an official's status was indicated by the number of carriages and horses which constituted his entourage. Models of these were placed in his tomb.

same time, however, the realism which can be seen in the art of the Qin became more widespread while, intellectually, an interest in popular beliefs, in shamanism and the like became respectable. These interests were reflected in art: Watson cites as instances of this the *boshanlu*, the incense burner in the shape of a cosmic mountain, and the so-called 'cloud-scroll', translating cosmic space into ornament.

The needs of the dead and the provision of grave goods furnish extensive evidence for the household objects as well as the beliefs of the Han and, to some extent, of the peoples living on the periphery of China, especially those in the southern regions. The continued preoccupation with the preservation of the body as a home for the *bo* led to increasingly complicated burial techniques: the results, in the absence of mummification in the Egyptian manner, were seldom satisfactory, but there were some remarkable exceptions.

Han Burials

There is a well-known story in the *History of the Three Kingdoms* that in the period A.D. 220-6 the people of Wu opened the tomb of Wu ruyi, king of Changsha who died in 202 B.C. They found the royal body intact, its clothes preserved. In appearance he was just like Wu Gan, a contemporary of the excavators, and he, it emerged, was a descendant, in the sixteenth generation, of the dead king. The tombs cut deep into the rock at Mancheng, Hebei, south-west of Beijing, where the jade suits were found, failed in their preservative intentions, but others at Mawangdui were remarkably successful. Here, in the eastern suburbs of Changsha the body of a princess was found in a surprising state of preservation. These and thousands of other graves which have been investigated since 1948 testify to the wealth and inventiveness of Han upper classes and those who served then, and they provide considerable evidence for their beliefs and ideas.

The royal burials in Shizhaishan, Yunnan, the graves of the rulers of Dian, show a fascinating mixture of objects of Chinese origin, whether acquired by trade or as gifts from the Han court before the annexation of the kingdom, others with very strong evidence for central Asian influences, and yet others which point to connections with the Dongson culture of south-east Asia. It is interesting to note that the realism which is so marked a feature of Han art, especially in its later phases, is already very strong at Shizhaishan. There is a rich animal repertory and evidence for a bird-snake theme, still to be found in the southern frontier region and widespread in south-east Asia where it become conflated with the Indian *garuda-naga* motif. Small bronze figurines of men and women assembled in groups on circular platforms set on drum-like supports, which also served as containers for cowries, were used to depict various scenes.

Left. A *wu* shaman or exorcist. Shamanism, the earliest form of cult in China, and relying on magic, was intended to give humans power over the gods. Its appeal was of longer duration and more popular than any of the philosophies, so that it gradually took over and transformed Daoism and Chinese Buddhism. Possibly from the Luoyang district, *c.* third century A.D. Seligman Collection.

Opposite. A bronze from Tomb 13, Shizhaishan, Yunnan, *c.* 100 B.C. The art of the kingdom of Dian contains many references to cattle, which obviously played a major role in the economy and in rituals. Another piece shows a sacrificial bull tied to an ornamented post. Sima Qian wrote of its inhabitants as semi-nomadic cattle-raisers, 'following their herds about'. Snakes and birds are other important elements in Dian symbolism and seem later to have been equated with the *garuda* and *naga* of Indian tradition. The bird-snake motif is still found among hill peoples in the border regions of southern China.

These included battles, sometimes between foot-soldiers and cavalry, rituals of offerings, men in various carefully distinguished tribal costumes taking animals to market, and apparently a human sacrifice. Other groups in a somewhat different style show bullfighting and men drinking from large ceremonial jars, a practice still to be seen in south-east Asian longhouses. A decorated bull attached to a post is clearly a sacrificial animal of the type still found in Laos in this century. Bronze ploughshares suggest ritual agriculture by the king or his substitute, such as the Thai rulers still practise and was once to be found in China also.

At about the time that the annexation of Dian was beginning the burials took place in Hebei of Prince Liu Sheng, a member of the imperial family who held the fief of Zhongshan and died in 113 B.C., and his wife, the princess Dou Wan. They were interred in two rock-cut tombs at Mancheng, about 90 miles (150 kilometres) south-west of Beijing. Excavations here produced almost 3000 objects to accompany the dead, whose bodies were encased in suits made out of thin jade tablets. Each suit consisted of more than 2000 pieces of jade, probably from Xinjiang, wired together to form boots, gloves, trousers, jacket and head-mask; this must have required thousands of hours by skilled lapidaries, vain work since the bodies decayed.

Those responsible for the tombs at Mawangdui were more successful, at least in the case of the Lady Xin Zhui who died some decades earlier. Her burial pit was surmounted by a mound of rammed earth, about 55 yards (50 metres) in diameter at the base and rising to a height of 22 yards (20 metres). The burial pit had a sloping entrance on the north side and was in the form of a rectangular funnel which narrowed in four stages until a slight enlargement at the bottom formed the burial chamber proper 8 by 7 yards (7 by 6 metres). This contained a vast outer coffin of wood, which was surrounded on all sides by great quantities of charcoal. Above this was a thick layer of white, sticky clay which closed the chamber itself. Above this, filling the shaft and funnel, were layers of hard rammed earth, about 19 inches (half a metre) thick, pounded with a small rammer which increased the density of the fill. These extraordinarily thorough preliminaries served to preserve the coffin and its content until its excavation in 1972.

The contents of Han Tomb No. 1, Mawangdui, though not the richest of Han tombs, are remarkable both for their state of preservation and their documentation. Three outer coffins and three inner, all in wood with scrupulous joinery, housed more than a thousand objects of silk, lacquer, bamboo, ceramics, cereals and other foodstuffs and the body of a fifty-year

old woman. This had been placed on its back, head to the north, in some twenty layers of clothing tied in silk ribbons at nine points and further covered with a painted gauze gown and another silk tabby one, both padded. A complete inventory of the tomb contents was written on 312 bamboo slips.

The greatest part of the *mingchi* (replicas made to serve as grave goods) were stowed in four spaces made between the outer and the middle coffins, but the most remarkable find was of a painting on silk which lay over the innermost casket, a kind of T-shaped banner which has been identified from the inventory as a *fei yi*, flying garment. It seems, among much else, to contain a portrait of the dead woman. But it is by no means the only painting in the burial chamber. The inside of the innermost coffin was painted with cinnabar lacquer. This housed the outermost casket whose walls were covered with a black lacquer ground on which white, black, red and yellow clouds swirl round grotesque figures. These fight, hunt, dance or play musical instruments, amid flying beasts. The whole is bordered with a geometric pattern. On the next casket, which has a red lacquer ground, the cover has swirling clouds with two tigers and two dragons fighting. The sides show mountains amid clouds with running deer, dragons, grotesque animals and *bi*-like discs, again with a geometric border. The design on each side is different. The innermost casket was covered in silk decorated with satin stitch and coloured feathers arranged in lozenges.

More than 180 brilliantly coloured and decorated lacquer vessels were found, many bearing the name of their owner, their use and often their capacity. Some contained the remains of food. There were 162 wooden mortuary figures, 36 small ones found in the space between the innermost casket and its surrounding one, the remainder in the storage space. The larger figures, some standing, some sitting, some in model clothes, others with painted attire, include some 23 who appear to represent a group of

musicians and dancers accompanied by small lacquered tables and screens and food trays, as if to make up a banquet for the tomb's occupant. A wooden zither, a mouth organ and a set of twelve pitch pipes with the tones marked in ink were also found. There was one bronze mirror. It seems likely that the smaller of the statuettes, tied together in two groups with hemp string, served to repel evil spirits, positioned as they were by the inmost casket.

It has been suggested that these mannikins were *tao ren*, peach men, whose function was to repel *guei*, wicked spirits. Their prototypes seem to have been Shen Tu and his younger brother Yu Lu. According to the later Han writer Wang Chong, whose book *Lun Heng* was designed to prove that Heaven did not interfere in the affairs of earth and of men, quoting a passage in the *Shanhaijing* which does not appear in the surviving text, these two spirits, *shen*, lived on Mount Du Xue.

There is a giant peach tree whose branches extend for three thousand *li* with a gate of demons, *guei men*, in its north-eastern tangle. This is on the route between heaven and earth for ten thousand spirits who were under the control of these two *shen* who sat

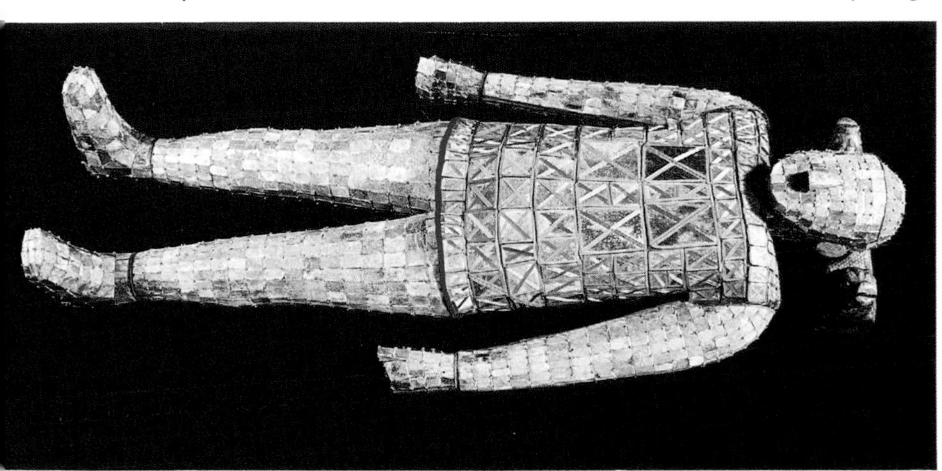

Left. Jade was found in burials in China from prehistoric times: it seems always to have been associated with ideas of immortality. The practice reaches its height towards the end of the second century B.C. at Mancheng, Hebei, when Prince Liu Sheng and his wife, Dou Wan, were placed in their rock-cut tombs in suits made of thousands of jade tablets stitched together with gold wire. The virtuosity of the jade-workers was remarkable, but they worked in vain: the bodies decayed.

Opposite above. Top of a bronze drum from Shizhaishan. In the grave it served as a container for cowries, which were used as currency. Drums of bronze were widely distributed in South East Asia, where they seem to have originated, but it is only in Yunnan, in the kingdom of Dian, that scenes using small bronze figurines of considerable naturalism are found on the tympana. Here a woman whose importance is indicated by her greater size is shown receiving presents set out on trays. Other women are shown weaving on simple waist-looms. Tomb 1, Shizhaishan: second to first century B.C.

Left. Parcel-gilt leopards from the tomb of Princess Dou Wan. There were four in all, probably securing the edges of the pall. Leopards, here magnificently inset with silver and garnets as befits the tomb of an emperor's daughter-in-law whose husband held the fief of Zhongshan, are found in various contexts in Han funerary rites. They guard the ramp which leads from the earthly level to the entrance to heaven and also the gateway of heaven itself, on the Mawangdui banner (see page 39). They are also found at Shizhaishan.

Below and opposite. Pottery tomb decorations of the Six Dynasties period (A.D. 479–581), showing female figures riding on the symbolic animals of the four cardinal directions, which grew from the dead Pangu and were ultimately derived from the principles of *yin* and *yang*. William Rockhill Nelson Gallery of Art, Kansas City, Missouri. Nelson Fund. *Below.* The Green Dragon of the east and of spring, whose element was wood. The dragon, as bringer of regenerating rain, embodied the *yang* principle, positive and male. *Bottom.* The Red Bird of the south, the phoenix or *feng-huang*, whose element was fire and whose season was summer. It symbolised drought and embodied the *yin* principle, negative and female. The phoenix represented the Empress, while the dragon stood for the Emperor. *Opposite above.* The White Tiger of the west, regarded as the king of beasts, whose season was autumn and whose element was metal. *Opposite below.* The Dark Warrior, a tortoise and a snake, associated with the north and with winter, whose element was water and whose colour was black.

Centre. Entrance to a burial chamber, Yangzishan, Sichuan. Such tombs, either in stone and brick or wholly in stone, were designed like dwelling places. The bronze animal masks, often depicting a bird surmounting a monster-head, which served to close the wooden doors in earlier tombs, are here replaced by an incised drawing in the stone of a head with a ring in its mouth surmounted by a bird. The tiger and dragon, below this motif on the right and left leaves of the door, are the animals of the directions and serve to locate the tomb in space. The fish incised on the lintel may symbolise longevity. Second century A.D.

above the gate. Those who had committed evil deeds were caught by the *shen*, bound with ropes and fed to tigers. (Because the *guei* had substance they were both caught and eaten.) Huang Di had a large peachwood man made and pictures of the two *shen* and the tigers painted on the leaves of the door of the gate of demons, together with ropes which hung on the doors, to repel the *guei*. Mount Du Xue was in the middle of the great sea, a position which may link it with Penglai, the island of the immortals.

The mannikins served, if this interpretation is correct, to protect the

occupant of the tomb from demons. They were placed outside the innermost casket where the *fei yi* lay above the body within. This was probably a guide to lead the *hun* soul of the Lady Xin Zhui to paradise through all the perils that threatened it en route, perils of which the songs of the South, the *Chu ci*, speak so dramatically.

The interpretation of the *fei yi* is still a matter for debate. The main points of contention have been summarised by Loewe, who has also advanced an interpretation of his own which seems acceptable in many respects. Briefly, the banner seems to represent the island of Penglai to which the lady's soul has already made its way. It shows her approach to the gate of heaven and a number of scenes or episodes with recognisably salvationist implications, which are discussed below. These include the gate of heaven itself whose porters eye the approaching soul 'churlishly'; the Fu Sang tree and the ten suns; the hare and the toad in the moon; the bird in the sun, and so on.

There was another development in Han times which had considerable importance. This was the growth of the doctrine of the Five Elements, first adumbrated in the third century B.C. *Taiji*, the Great Ultimate, gave rise to *yin-yang* whose interaction produced the *wu xing* (the Five Phases), the Five Elements whose continuing interaction as an eternal cycle can be used to explain the constant fluctuations in the relationships of the triad of heaven, human beings and earth, which constitutes the unity that is the universe.

These five elements also furnish what may be called the building blocks of the universe. Their interaction can be symbolised as water, fire, metal, wood, earth; these are assigned to directions (and hence to the animals that symbolise them: north

to serpent/turtle, called the dark warrior; south to vermilion bird; west to white tiger; east to green dragon). Earth is centre and has no animal but may be represented by the *zong* or the round boss in a square frame at the centre of a bronze mirror. Water extinguishes fire which melts metal which destroys wood which overcomes earth which absorbs water. Water is linked with winter and the planet Mercury; fire with Mars and summer; metal with autumn and Venus; wood with Jupiter and spring; earth with Saturn: there is no fifth season. Wood and fire are the rising and mature power of *yang*: metal and water the rise and maturity of *yin*. Earth symbolises a state of equilibrium.

The endless permutations of these and dozens of other pentads could be called into aid to support any number of philosophical and metaphysical systems and to explain the general concept of *dao* as natural order and not simply connected with Daoism. These ideas also furnish topics for the scenes which are depicted in the reliefs and paintings on the walls of Han tombs, the decorations on lacquers and bronzes, either by themselves or in combination with myths from the past, reconstructions by Confucian scholars and elements of popular traditions.

Left. Guan Zhong, one of the generals in the period known as the Three Kingdoms, which in the second century A.D. brought the Han dynasty to an end in a period of disorder similar to that which ushered it in. Guan Zhong was later deified as Guan Di, god of war. Rubbing from stone engraving. British Museum, London.

Previous pages, left. The paintings which have survived on the walls of Han tombs give some indication of what has been lost with the destruction of the palaces and halls of emperors and nobles whose walls were covered with paintings, where, in the words of a contemporary poet, the artist had shaped truly and carefully all the wonders of life.

Previous pages, right. The *fei yi*, flying banner, from the tomb of the Lady Xin Zhui, a painting on silk. There is general agreement that the purpose of this remarkable object, one of the earliest surviving paintings from China, was to guide the *hun* soul of the princess to paradise: other offerings in the tomb were intended to placate the *po* soul so that it would remain on good terms with the living and help in communications with the ancestors. The exact interpretation of the complex symbolism remains a matter for argument and discussion. Mawangdui, Tomb 1, Changsha, Hunan, *c.* 186 B.C.

The Myths and Their Sources

A fundamental problem confronts every student of Chinese mythology. We are lucky that we possess a vast body of Chinese literature and historical material, a corpus of written sources more ancient and continuous than for any other people. But although much of it purports to belong to the period of Shang and Zhou – the archaeological record of which we have already considered – this is not actually the case. Texts abound, and all have their commentaries and comments upon the commentators. But the greater part of these are compilations of a much later date than appears at first sight, generally Han, though often incorporating considerable amounts of much older material. And such compilations are usually the work of scholars who used supposedly old and traditional material to sustain their own viewpoints by giving them an air of historical legitimacy.

Li Si and the Burning of Books

A number of the best-known Chinese philosophers lived in the period of the Warring States when, we may assume, some of the feudal traditions and practices were still living. But already Chinese society was in a state of flux and one has the impression that such scholars as Confucius were attempting to restore an imaginary status quo in reaction to the social changes amidst which they were living and which they deplored. Some evidence in support of this view can be found in Sima Qian's account of a proposal made in 213 B.C. by Li Si, minister of Shi Huang Di. Li Si is execrated among scholars for his proposal, which the emperor accepted, for the burning of all books, save technical manuals and handbooks; and it is partly as a result of his action that we are so inadequately furnished with early Chinese myths and legends. His proposal is of value, however, in setting out clearly the attitude of the scholar class and serves to explain, in our present context, some of the reasons why post-Qin texts must be viewed with scepticism as original source material. For what was reconstructed tended to reflect a highly selective version of tradition, favourable largely to the *junzi* scholar class. Li Si's memorial went as follows:

The Five Emperors did not copy each other, the Three Dynasties did not imitate their predecessors. Each had its own particular form of government. It was not that they were opposed to the methods of their predecessors but that times had changed. Now Your Majesty has brought about a great achievement, and founded a glory that will last for ten thousand years. But, narrow-minded scholars cannot understand this. The proposals of Shunyu are based upon practices in the Three Dynasties, but why should we take them as a model? [Shunyu, a conservative minister, had argued in favour of re-establishing a system of fiefs, on the grounds that they had always existed.] *The princes used always to be at war. They paid much attention to itinerant scholars and relied on their advice. But now the realm has been pacified and law and order emanates from a single authority. The common people are engaged upon industry and agriculture while the superior people study law and administration. Only the scholars fail to conform to the new trends and study the past in order to deprecate the present. They*

Below centre. Solid bronze plaque depicting a leaping tiger. The incised decoration suggests wings; the tiger, which in the autumn descended from the mountains in the west, was associated with the autumn and the west and, though known to the Chinese, was often treated as a fabulous beast. Zhou dynasty. British Museum, London.

Opposite left. A phoenix or *feng-huang*, emblem of the south, of the *yin* principle and of the empress, which in popular mythology was believed to mark buried treasure. One of a pair of phoenixes in thin gold sheet. Tang dynasty. Seattle Art Museum, Washington. Eugene Fuller Memorial Collection.

Opposite right. Goddess holding the *juyi*, the Precious Stone of the Pearly Emperor Yu-huang. The crayfish on which she stands is, like all fish, an emblem of wealth, regeneration, harmony and connubial bliss. British Museum, London.

Below. A *long*, or dragon, which was regarded as a beneficent spirit of the moist, *yang* principle, dwelling in the clouds or the waters. There were five sorts: heavenly, which guarded the mansions of the gods; spiritual, which controlled winds and rains, and only accidentally cause flooding; earthly, which cleared rivers and deepened seas; those of hidden treasure; and imperial, marked by five claws, the others having four. Porcelain dish, region of Kang Xi. Metropolitan Museum of Art, New York. Bequest of Michael Friedsam, 1932.

cause doubts and misgivings among the black-haired [the people – the usual phrase for the peasantry]. *The Counsellor, your servant Li Si, aware that in offering incorrect advice he may incur the death penalty, proposes as follows. In the past the realm was divided and troubled: none could unite it. Many princes ruled at the same time. Scholars rely in their discussions upon the old times in order to decry the present and use false instances to create confusion in current matters. They proclaim the excellence of what they have studied in order to denigrate the achievements of Your Majesty. Now that the whole realm is in the hands of a single ruler, they praise the past and keep themselves aloof. When they hear of a new edict, they criticise it in the light of their researches for they oppose new laws and orders. At Court they are discreet, but elsewhere they indulge in public debate and encourage the common people to believe their calumnies. This being so, if no action is taken, the imperial authority will be diminished, and the power of the dissident will increase. This must be prevented. Your servant proposes that the Histories, save that of Qin, shall be burnt. Except for those of the rank of Scholar of Great Learning* [of whom there were only 70] *everyone throughout the realm who possesses a copy of the Shu jing, the Shi jing and the works of the Hundred Schools* [of philosophy] *must take them to the magistrates to be burnt. Those who dare to discuss or comment upon the Shu jing and the Shi jing shall be put to death and their bodies exposed in the market place. Those who laud ancient institutions to the disparagement of the present regime shall be exterminated with their families. Officials who condone breaches of this order shall be treated as accomplices. Anyone who has not burnt his books within thirty days of this order shall be branded and sent to forced labour at the Great Wall. Only those books which treat of medicine, divination, agriculture and arboriculture shall be allowed. Those who wish to study law and administration may do so by modelling*

Above. Scholars studying the symbols of *yin* and *yang*, the cardinal principles of the universe which philosophers tried to bring into harmony and which were basic to so much Chinese mystical symbolism. Their effort to seek out first causes made the scholars seem obscurantist troublemakers to Li Si. Seventeenth century. British Museum, London.

Above right. Detail from a Han pottery tile depicting the legendary meeting of Laozi and Confucius. Confucius lived from 551 to 479 B.C. The actual existence of Laozi is less certain, but his followers claimed that he lived around 590 B.C. His philosophy was, like Confucianism, a reaction to troubled times. Musée Cernuschi, Paris.

Opposite. The Seven Sages of the Bamboo Grove, a group of Daoist scholars living in the late third century A.D. who, rejecting Confucian orthodoxy and equally the magical practices of the *wu* shamans, developed Zhuangzi's philosophy of non-action. They were ridiculed as eccentric drunkards and persecuted for their unwillingness to bend philosophy to support the changing dynasties. Silk tapestry of the late eighteenth century.

themselves upon officials of the government.

There is no doubt of the reality of the destruction, as the deaths of 460 scholars on charges of concealing books testify. That so much survived is a tribute to the scholars who were the object of Li Si's attack; that so much of what survives belongs to the Confucian school demonstrates how widely that particular school of philosophy had spread. The decree none the less broke the continuity of tradition and it is clear, for example from the work of Sima Qian, that much difficulty was experienced in understanding parts of the ancient literature which had been laboriously reconstructed under the Han. Sima Qian appears to have totally failed to understand the distinction, critically important for a grasp of the power structure in feudal China, between clan and family names. As has been remarked by a western scholar of the period: 'So completely had the aristocracy lost caste and position at the end of the revolution that a scholar and a conservative no longer clearly understood that their ancient privileges had been founded on noble descent and not on education.'

The Fall of Qin

Although the decree ended the hope of those who wished to restore the feudal system, it also brought about the end of Qin nobility; scholars and peasants alike united in their hatred of the Qin military overlords, whose oppression seemed far more onerous than that of the feudal lords of the past. As a Han scholar wrote:

From princes and ministers to the humblest of the people all were terrified and went in fear of their lives. No man was secure in office: all were liable to degradation. Thus Chen She [a commoner and soldier from Chu who initiated the first mutiny against Qin Shi Huang Di's successor] *without needing to be a sage like Tang or Wu* [who founded the Shang and Zhou dynasties], *without having any high rank . . . had only to wave his arms for the whole realm to answer like an echo. When a man has the rank of Son of Heaven and all the wealth of the realm as his resources and yet cannot escape slaughter it is because he has failed to distinguish between the means by which power is maintained safely and the causes of disaster.*

The revolt which Chen She initiated was suppressed, but many further rebellions followed and it is interesting to note that each of the groups tended to set up its independent king in the old tradition, their candidates being obscure members of the old royal families. Ultimately two leaders emerged, Liu Bang a commoner and future founder of the Han dynasty, and Xiang You, a Chu aristocrat who was also a hereditary general.

At first the aristocrat appeared

V.A.M.

quite successful. He set up a state in which territories were distributed to various of his supporters and to Qin generals who had changed sides. Liu Bang was granted a realm in Sichuan and parts of Shaanxi, known as Han from the local river. The feudal system which Xiang You tried to re-establish proved quite unequal to the problems of the new state, in which he ruled as Ba Wang or supreme king. Bloody fighting broke out between the various holders of land, but in the end this resolved itself into a struggle between Liu Bang and Xiang You. The war lasted five years and ended in victory for Liu Bang, who established his capital at Xian in Shaanxi. As emperor he took the name Gaozu in 202 B.C.

Gaozu gave fiefs to his followers but reserved the title of king for members of his own family, none the less appointing imperial officers to oversee their rule. His victorious generals were gradually deprived of the lands which they had received as reward for their support and most were degraded in rank: many were put to death. One of his successors had the ingenious idea of making all the sons of a feudal lord his coheirs. As a result the number of fiefs increased, since the lands held had to be fragmented to meet the demands of the heirs, but each fief became less and less significant with every succeeding generation.

Finally, Gaozu and his successors employed the strongest advocates of theoretical feudalism, the old scholar class, to justify the idea that all were subservient to the state in the person of the ruler.

Confucianism Rewritten

The books which had been destroyed under Shi Huang Di were now reconstructed but re-interpreted to provide a picture of the past in which the feudal period was seen as a degenerate phase in a once unified empire which the Han dynasty had now restored. The works of Confucius which had been devised as a codification of aristocratic ethics were now extended to furnish a universal system. The interpretation and maintenance of this system were to be the function of the scholar class, whose status depended upon education not, as in the time of Confucius, upon birth.

The decree promoted by Li Si was repealed in 191 B.C. though it had not been enforced since the fall of the Qin dynasty. Han scholars set about the reconstruction of the texts which had been destroyed, and since they were mainly followers of Confucius it was the works of that sage and those who were considered as of his school which received the main attention. These books are what are usually referred to as 'the Classics'. Among the most important is the *Shu jing*, the Book of Documents. Of this there are two texts: one, the so-called 'old' text, was alleged to have been found hidden in the wall of Confucius's own house and edited by one of his descendants, Kong Anguo. The other, the 'modern' text (the epithet refers to the new style of calligraphy in which it was written), was preserved by Fu Sheng, who had been a member of the Academy set up under Li Si's decree and was said to have written down 29 chapters by heart. (In another version he too had hidden his text in the wall of his house during the persecutions under Shi Huang Di.) The *Shu jing* consists of documents, speeches, proclamations and orations belonging to various historical or pseudo-historical events. Another work is the *Shi jing* or Book of Songs, an anthology of ancient poems which caused much trouble to Confucian scholars since their subjects, often frank accounts of sexual licence and desire, had to be interpreted in political and ethical terms. The *I jing* or Book of Changes is a divination manual in two parts. The first section consists of rhymed traditional lore, typical of peasant lore throughout the world. The second part is a handbook, depending largely upon interpretations of the *ba gua*, the eight trigrams, to deal with formulae of the kind also associated with the oracle bones mentioned already. The method of employing the *ba gua* is attributed to Wen, the father of the first Zhou king, Wu. The *Li ji*, Book of Rites, and the *Zhou Li*, Zhou Ritual, are both manuals. The latter purports to be a manual of Zhou ritual although in fact it was compiled in the third century B.C. when Zhou was already a spent force. The *Li ji* was compiled by Dai the Younger about 50 B.C. but the earliest elements included may date from the time of the Confucian Analects, that is from before 450 B.C. These are what Karlgren has called systematising texts: their function is not to record but to set out, in the tradition of the Confucian scholars who compiled and reconstructed them, what the rites should be, not what they actually were.

There are other textual sources. Of these one, the *Chunqin*, Spring and Autumn Annals, is a history of the state of Lu from 722 to 481 B.C. and wrongly attributed by orthodox

Opposite. Guan Di, who combined the functions of god of war with those of god of literature. Guan Di was a civilising deity who could avert war and uphold justice. Screen painting, nineteenth century. Victoria and Albert Museum, London.

Below. Confucius, whose works upholding the aristocratic order to which he belonged were reinterpreted under the Han to support the ruling Son of Heaven and to justify the power of the current dynasty in terms of tradition. The scholar class itself stood to benefit from the resurgence of the great philosopher. Statuette showing him dressed as a mandarin. Late Ming/early Qing. Musée Guimet, Paris.

Left. Fuxi, first of the Three Sovereigns and supposed inventor of the *ba gua*, the eight trigrams, which lie on the ground before him. In addition to their role in divination the *ba gua* were the basis of Chinese calligraphy, so scholars especially revered Fuxi who, despite his 'archaic' dress, is seen with the long nails worn by scholars. The tortoise before him is a reminder that tortoise shells were used as oracle bones. Portrait by Ma Lin. Song dynasty. National Palace Museum, Taipei

Opposite. Daoist priest's robe of brocade embroidered with the eight trigrams, which were linked with the five elements, earth, metal, water, wood, fire and, in the centre, the interlocked symbols of *yin* and *yang*. *Yin* and *yang* and their manifestation in the elements were thought from late Zhou times to constitute the *Dao* or Way, the principle of the universe, and were the basis of court ritual. Eighteenth to nineteenth century. Metropolitan Museum of Art, New York.

Confucian scholars to the master himself. The work is a dull but apparently accurately dated chronicle; there is every reason to believe that it was paralleled in all the other states. A rather more lively account of history in the feudal period is to be found in the *Zuo zhuan*, which incorporates a brief ritual commentary on the *Chunqin*. The *Zuo zhuan* is a compilation, attributed to the writer Zuo Shi (*c.* 330 B.C.) but in fact a composite work of various dates from about 430 B.C. to the middle of the third century B.C. with amendments and additions attributable to Confucian scholars of Qin and Han times. This is a valuable source for mythology, but its versions of myths and legends must be treated as the products of Confucian editing.

Other Philosophical Schools

Of the non-Confucian schools there is very little that has survived from early times. The Legalist school is represented by the *Shang Zhun Zhu*, the work of a member of the princely house of Wei who flourished in the mid-fourth century B.C., and the philosopher Han Fei Zi, of the following century. Both incorporate traditions from the early period of Chinese history which reflect ideas

Left. Earthenware censer recovered from a well in the Yellow Temple, Beijing. The vessel, built up from moulded earthenware sections, consists of a tripod supporting bowl surmounted by a mountain and a dragon. The piece, which was used as an incense-burner, is unique. It has been described as standing for 'Confucian traditionalism'. Yuan dynasty (A.D. 1260-1368).

Below. Part of the Nine Dragon scroll, painted in 1244 by the Daoist poet and painter Chenrong, which shows the manifestation of dragons from the ocean waves and from the clouds. Besides being the auspicious bringers of rain and the symbol of the emperor, dragons, according to the Daoists, were symbolic of the Way, the central truth of their philosophy, which revealed itself momentarily only to vanish in mystery. Museum of Fine Arts, Boston, Massachusetts. Francis Gardner Curtis Fund.

outside the canons of Confucian orthodoxy. Another valuable source for such matters is the work of the Daoist writer Zhuangzi, who is perhaps best known for his discussion of the problem of knowledge:

Once Zhuang dreamed that he was a butterfly, fluttering about enjoying himself. The butterfly did not know that it was Zhuang. Then it awoke and was truly Zhuang again. But I do not know whether it was then Zhuang dreaming he was a butterfly or whether I am now a butterfly, dreaming that I am Zhuang.

Those concerned with Chinese mythography must often have somewhat similar sensations of doubt.

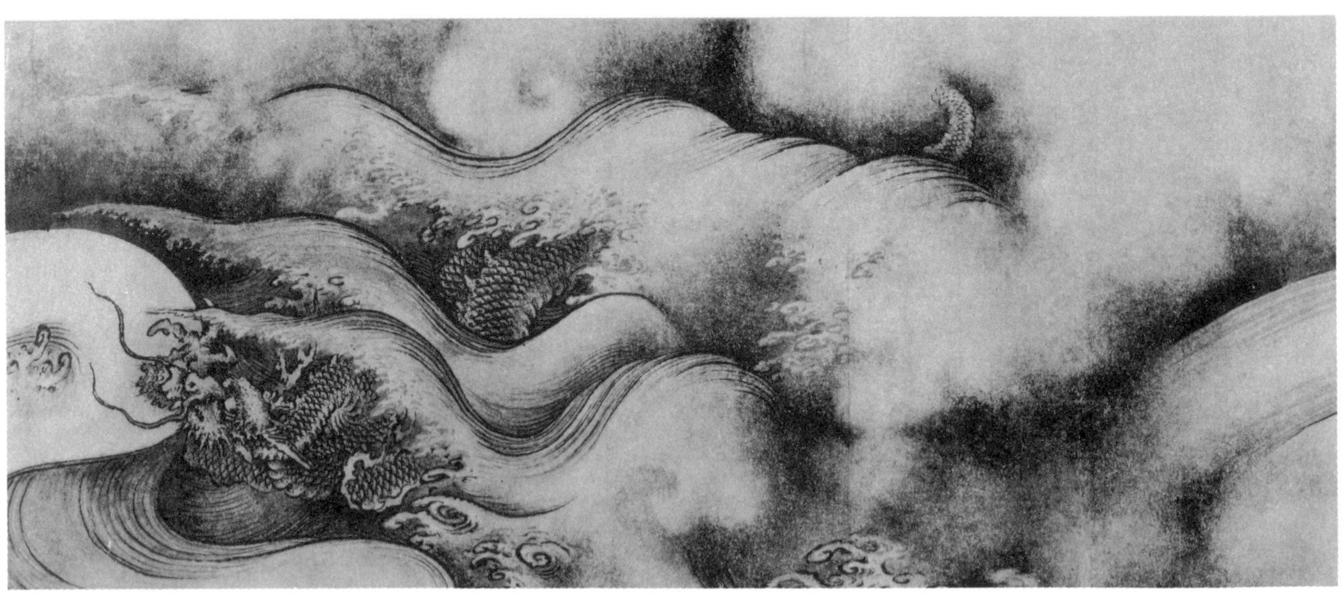

The Creation of the World

Most, if not all, mythologies include an account of the creation of the world and its inhabitants, both human and animal, together with some explanation of the origins of their natural setting. That such accounts can be found in Chinese is true, but what we have is rudimentary and gives every appearance of being the product of scholarly compilers who were, generally, concerned to recount cosmogonies as parables to illustrate philosophical theories. The most extensive account of the creation, involving a giant called Pangu, has survived only in texts from the third to sixth centuries A.D., and there is good reason to think that this story was not incorporated into Chinese tradition until after the assimilation of the southern region. There are, on the other hand, accounts of the structure of the world – rather than of its creation, which seems to have interested the Chinese much less – which are older than the Pangu myth and seem to belong to an original Chinese tradition. These we shall consider later, but first we must examine what there is of a creation story.

Order from Chaos

Philosophically, for the Chinese as for other people, creation was the act of reducing chaos to order, a theme which persists throughout Chinese thought. For the essence of good rule is that Heaven and Earth shall be in accord and the rites observed. The best-known allegory of the ending of Chaos is to be found in the work of Zhuangzi (third century B.C.), who tells how Hu, the emperor of the Northern Sea, and Shu, the emperor of the Southern Sea, used from time to time to meet half way between their respective domains, that is on the territory of the emperor of the Centre, Hundun. Hundun was most hospitable, but was distinguished from other men by the fact that he lacked the seven orifices, for seeing, hearing, eating and breathing. Wishing to repay him for his kindness, Shu and Hu decided that they would bore the necessary holes in Hundun and this they did at the rate of one hole a day. But on the seventh day Hundun, whose name means Chaos, died. At the same moment the world came into being. There is an interesting additional turn to the story, since the combined names of the two other emperors, Shu-hu, mean lightning, and there is a hint that it is the lightning which strikes Chaos and destroys it so that the world may emerge.

Soymié has noted that in certain ritual transpositions lightning is represented by burning arrows directed at a goatskin bottle which may have represented chaos. There are two curious stories concerned with the fate of the Shang dynasty and the end of the dynastic line in which the theme of shooting at a sack is to be found. The first of these concerns King Wuyi, who made a figure in human shape and called it Tianshen, spirit of Heaven. He then played *qi* (a board game of the draughts or checkers type) with the figure, whose pieces were moved by a man appointed to the task by the king. There is no mention of the stake, but the victorious king mocked and abused the figure. He then made a sack of skin, filled it with blood and, having had it hung up, shot arrows at it, saying that he was shooting at Heaven. According to the *Shu jing*, where this story is found, Wuyi subsequently went on a hunting trip, was struck by lightning and killed.

This inevitably recalls the tradition implicit in the story that Shu-hu Lightning destroyed Hundun Chaos and thereby brought order into the world. There is some evidence that the popular name for a leather bottle *chiyi* was *hundun* and in view of the fact that, as we shall see below, Hundun was sometimes conceived of as a bird, we should note that the word *chi* means owl.

Hundun is also conceived of in human form, as a wicked son of the Yellow Emperor, Huang Di, who sends him into exile; in other texts there is a tradition that the exiling of Hundun was an act of the ruler Shun, just before he handed over power to Yu the Great, the founder of the Xia dynasty. Others say that the expulsion of Hundun and three associates whose virtue was exhausted took place as Yao handed over power to Shun. A decline in virtue leads to a world in chaos.

Yet another version is to be found in the *Shanhaijing*, the Hill and River Classic, where Hundun is a mythical bird like a yellow bag. (This links the creature both with Huang Di, the Yellow Emperor, father of one Hundun, and with the idea of Hundun as a sack.) At the same time, its colour is red like fire. It has six feet and four wings, but lacks a face – that is, lacks the seven openings. It can dance and can sing despite the absence of a mouth, and lives on the Mountain of the Sky which is rich in ores and in jade. A river rises here, in the west, which flows into the Hot Springs Valley in the east where the Fu Sang tree grows. And, because the Yellow Emperor is the emperor of the Centre in various cardinal systems as was Hundun in the story with which we started, he too is sometimes considered to be Chaos. In another text, Hundun is described as lacking the five viscera, although he has a stomach.

A more important tradition, however, links the seven openings with the supposed seven openings of the heart, whose possession was the mark of an upright person. It is recorded of Zhou Xin, the last ruler of the Shang dynasty and a paradigm of cruelty and vice, that he was reproved by his uncle Prince Bigan for his evil government. Zhou Xin replied: 'It is said that you are a sage and I have heard that a sage has seven openings to his heart.' He then had Bigan slain and his heart torn out to see whether it was true.

A further point of interest is that the last of Wuyi's lineage, Yen, the feudal prince of Song, arrogated to himself the title of king. He was finally defeated by the state of Qi and its allies, Wei and Chu. And of him we are told by Sima Qian that 'he filled a leather bottle with blood, hung it up and shot arrows against it, saying that he was shooting at Heaven'. With his defeat in 282 B.C. the last vestiges of Shang power came to an end. Now in recounting the fate of Yen, Sima Qian recalled the story of

Above. Yao, fourth of the Five Emperors. He was famed for his benign rule. With the help of Yi the Divine Archer, he subdued the unruly winds and with the help of Kun he attempted to quell the floodwaters of the Yellow River. When Yao resolved to pass his throne to Shun rather than to his own son, the ten suns appeared together and nearly destroyed the world. Painting on silk of the Qian Long period (1736-95). Metropolitan Museum of Art, New York. Gift of Mrs Edward S. Harkness, 1947.

Right. Huang Di, the Yellow Emperor, discussing with Shennong his classic book on medicine, supposed to contain the secret of immortality which he had learned from Taiyi. The pill of immortality also conferred the ability to make gold, and to obtain it was the aim of many Chinese emperors. Figures carved in ivory. Wellcome Institute for the History of Medicine, London.

Opposite. Shang or early Zhou wine vessel in the shape of an owl. Owls seem to have been of mythological significance from the earliest times. As nocturnal creatures they represented the dark, negative *yin* elements of the universe, and may well have symbolised Chaos, *hundun*, which had to be destroyed to bring order into the world. Minneapolis Institute of Arts, Minnesota. Bequest of Alfred F. Pillsbury.

Wuyi (as well as that of Jie, the tyrannical last ruler of Xia). This seems to indicate that it was the presumption of challenging Heaven which led to the defeat (or destruction) of Yen as it had to that of his remote ancestor Wuyi. Yen shot arrows at those who criticised him, according to Sima Qian. This was the same as shooting

arrows at Heaven since, in Granet's opinion, the people represent Heaven.

According to a text of the third century A.D., Chaos was like a hen's egg. At this time neither Earth nor Heaven existed. From this egg, Pangu was born. The parts of the egg separated, the heavy elements forming the Earth, and the light, pure ones the Sky. These were *yin* and *yang*. For a period of eighteen thousand years the distance between earth and sky increased by 10 feet (3 metres) daily and Pangu grew at the same rate, so that his body always filled the space between the two. Despite this, when Pangu is represented, it is as a dwarf clad either in a bearskin or in leaves. On his death, the various parts of his body became different natural elements, though the exact details of these changes vary from text to text and from period to period. Thus in Han or even slightly earlier sources, his head became the Mountain of the East, his stomach the Mountain of the Centre, his left arm that of the South, his right arm that of the North and his feet that of the West. Another source derives all the cardinal mountains from his head and makes the sun and moon from his eyes, the rivers and seas from his flesh, the plants from his hair. Other theoreticians explained that his tears were the source of rivers and seas, his breath the wind, his eyes lightning and his voice thunder. Yet another story explained changes in the weather by changes in his mood. The most detailed version of this process of transformation is even more specific. His breath became wind and clouds, his voice thunder and lightning; his left eye was the sun, his right the moon; from his body the cardinal points and the five great mountains derived, while his blood and bodily fluids made the rivers and seas and his nervous and venous systems the layers of the earth. The fields and soil were the transformation of his flesh. The hairs of his head and eyebrows became the stars and planets, while metals and stones were

Right. Stylised tortoise, a symbol of stability, holding up the foundations of the universe. Originally a link between heaven and earth, the pillar was later thought to keep them apart. Probably *c.* eighteenth century A.D., based on a Ming style. Fogg Art Museum, Cambridge, Massachusetts.

Opposite. The fairy Magu, said to live in the second century A.D., was a beneficent sorceress who reclaimed from the sea a large area of the coast of Jiangsu and converted it into a mulberry orchard. In another avatar she took pity on her father's labourer, quarrelling with her father as a result and fleeing to the mountains to become a hermit. Painting by Xiang Gun. British Museum, London.

Below. Pangu, bearing in his hands the egg of Chaos, which is composed of the symbols of *yin* and *yang*, and from which he was born. Pangu lived for eighteen thousand years, growing at the rate of 10 feet (3 metres) a day and filling the space between Heaven and Earth. Nineteenth-century lithograph. British Museum, London.

the products of his teeth and bones; his semen became pearls, his bone-marrow jade. His sweat was the rain and the fleas on his body became the human race.

These stories are late in the versions in which we have them and it is likely that the tradition of their southern origin is basically correct, though there are elements in them which seem to fit the cosmogony of Zhuangzi. Chaos must end before the world begins. Similarly the concept of a pillar which keeps apart (or joins) the two parts of the world is found in Chinese cosmographical systems. There is also a tradition that there was a communicating link between Heaven and Earth until Shang Di ordered Chongli, a culture hero, to destroy it. The separation of chaos into an initial *yin* and *yang* is to be found as a fundamental concept in Chinese thought, perhaps reflected in a tradition from the region around the Yangtze delta that *yin* and *yang* derive from Pangu and his wife. There is some indication, though it is very imprecise, that at one time *yin* and *yang*, which are generally thought of as classificatory categories or abstract cosmic forces, may have had a more concrete form. There is a single reference to them as *shen* deities, responsible for the management of Earth and Heaven.

The concept of the world egg is not confined to China, nor that of the primordial being from whom all else is derived. In classical Indian cosmogonies a world egg occurs which opens to form the heavens from its upper part, earth from its lower. Brahma, the creator, emerged from this egg, and by incantation produced eight celestial elephants from part of the egg, to stand at the quarters and the four mid-points to hold earth and sky apart. There is also an Indian tradition, recorded in a very late

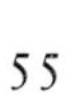

hymn of the *Rig Veda*, that the whole of creation derives from the primordial giant, Purusha, who is also the sacrifice of the gods. The Brahmin caste emerged from his mouth, the Kshatriya (warrior) caste from his arms, the Vaisya (merchants) from his thighs, the Sudra from his feet. From him also some of the gods were born, while from his navel came the air, from his head the sky and from his ears the four quarters. Though one story in the *Upanishads* states that the creature from which all emerged was a sacrificial horse, another upanishadic source has a single creator, a male, who divided himself into a male and female self. Approaching the female self he begat men. Then the creative pair assumed the forms of all creatures in turn and begat each of them. Stones of a single source splitting into a male and a female half which subsequently create by intercourse are not rare in south east Asia. In China the invention of marriage is attributed to a brother-sister pair. In a late story Tianlong and Diya are responsible for creating men and all other creatures sexually. It is not possible to say whether these parallels are the result of direct influences between India and China or represent traditions deriving from a common source. It should be noted, however, that many of the Chinese stories are late and may owe something to the Indian influences at the time when Buddhist pilgrims and scholars maintained contact with Indian intellectual circles.

We have already mentioned a tradition that when Pangu was happy the weather was fine, but when he grew angry the weather changed to fit his mood. There is a considerably more complicated account of the origins of climatic change, the cycle of seasons and day and night to be found in the *Shanhaijing*. A horned monster Gong-gong, having failed in an attempt to overthrow one of the Five Emperors, impaled Mount Buzhou, the north-west pillar of the universe. The act not only gave rise to a great flood (see page 88) but also tore a hole in the sky. In the absence of sky, the sun is unable to shine there, and instead there is a flaming dragon. This creature has a human face and a dragon's body a thousand *li* in length. Its colour is red, its eyes fixed. When its eyes are open, it is day; when they are closed, it is night. Its exhalation is winter; its inhalation is summer. When it stops breathing, there is neither rain nor wind; when it resumes breathing, the wind blows. It neither eats nor drinks. To the story of Gong-gong we return in the next section, for it is more properly concerned with the structure of the cosmos. What is interesting here is to see how the consequences of Gong-gong's act are used as a logical base for another, quite different story which 'explains' another set of phenomena.

Above. A jade *zong*, symbol of the square earth, whose central cylinder may originally have been designed to hold ancestral tablets, perhaps in the form of phallic symbols. Carved in incorruptible jade, *zongs* were in burials placed on the stomach of the deceased, the stomach of Pangu being the origin of the Mountain of the Centre, the fifth 'direction', whose colour was yellow and whose element was earth. Han dynasty. Museum Rietberg, Zurich.

Opposite. Cosmological chart showing strong Indian influence but preserving the Chinese notion of a chariot-like universe, with a central support and subsidiary guy ropes. British Museum, London.

The Creation of the Human Race

Although Chinese mythology has not much to say on creation in general – cosmogonies do not appear to have interested those who preserved early traditions or the scholars who speculated upon so much else – it might be expected that the creation of the human race itself would have seemed a theme of more importance. But this is not the case. We have already noted a late story, almost certainly a literary invention, that people were born of the parasites upon the body of the dead Pangu. The only other legend of any extent concerned with human creation presents the creator as the goddess Nugua, who is sometimes treated as the wife of Fuxi (see page 88), and who as a divine being attempted to repair the damage done by Gong-gong. According to a Han dynasty text, after Heaven and Earth had separated, there were still no people. Nugua set about modelling these out of yellow earth. But this process seemed too tedious and so the goddess took a rope and dipped it into the mud and trailed it about so that drops fell off. From the modelled specimens came the noble and rich, while those who dripped from the muddy rope were the humble and poor.

A folktale of quite uncertain date, recorded in Hebei, succeeds in conflating the idea of Pangu as the origin if not the creator of the human race and that of Nugua as the creator. In this story, once Earth and Heaven had evolved, and plants and animals had sprung up, Pangu was dissatisfied because there was no reasoning being who could develop and utilise other living creatures, these being incapable of any action on their own account. He therefore set about modelling men and women in clay. This took him a whole day. As soon as they were dry, they were impregnated with *yin* and *yang* and became human beings. Pangu had made a large supply which was baking in the sun when dark clouds appeared in the north-west (the region where the sun was unable to shine in the story). Fearful that his day's work might be wasted, Pangu heaped up the figures and carried

them indoors on an iron fork. But a great storm burst before he got them to safety and some were damaged. That is why there are crippled and defective people on earth.

There are other stories in which men and women are the product of sexual intercourse between a couple – often incestuous. Nugua herself is treated as a brother-sister pair in one version. Another couple, attendants of the god of Literature Wenchang, are Tianlong and Diya, who is also known as Dimu (that is, Earth-mother). From the union of this last couple not only human beings but all creation are said to have emerged.

The Structure of the Physical World

From sources which in the main date from the later part of the Han dynasty we can reconstruct some notion of the ideas which pre-Qin cosmographers entertained about the structure of the universe. Of the three cosmographical schools which appear to have existed, one called *suan ye* has left no body of doctrine, though it is known that its followers did not believe that the sky was solid, but that the sun and other heavenly bodies moved freely about in it. Of the other two schools considerably more is known and it will be no surprise to learn that the views which they held were completely incompatible.

One, which seems to show signs of a connection with the Pangu myth, went by the name of *hun-tian* and conceived of the world as a hen's egg with the long axis as the vertical. The upper part of the shell had the sky on its inner surface, across which the stars moved. The earth floated upon the primeval ocean, which lay in the bottom of the shell. Tidal influences accounted for the earth's seasons. There is no elaboration of the details about the ocean.

It seems most likely that the third school represented the oldest tradition or certainly one older than the *hun-tian* concept. For the supporters of this third school, known as *tian-gai* or *zhou-bei*, the sky was an inverted bowl, rotating on its own axis above the earth. The axis was the Pole Star, which carried with it the other

Left. Detail of a silk robe which belonged to the dowager Qing empress Ci-xi. The phoenix was, as is usual, identified with south, fire and *yang* at its zenith, appropriately enough for an empress. Nineteenth century. Metropolitan Museum of Art, New York.

Opposite. Detail of an emperor's marriage robe, showing the five-clawed imperial *long* (dragon), a rain-spirit which symbolised the emperor himself, and three of the twelve imperial symbols: above, the constellations, to which the emperor made offerings at the Altar of Heaven; left, the *fu* symbol of happiness; right, the axe symbolising the power to punish. Nineteenth century. Victoria and Albert Museum, London.

stars, fixed to the surface of the bowl. The earth was a flat surface or a truncated four-sided pyramid with the four seas set one on each of its sides. The notion of the earth's surface as square is old in the Chinese system of writing, while the term for space defined by the cardinal points, *yang*, also means square. The sun (or its deity) is represented by a square mound; the capital is square, as is the royal domain, and space can be seen as squares fitting about one another over a common centre or as juxtaposed lesser squares related to minor centres. Earth is still and square, while the round sky revolves: the *yang* sky contrasts with the *yin* earth.

The bowl of the *zhou-bei* system was conceived of as solid: when Gong-gong attacked it, he tore a hole so that the sun could no longer visit the north-west section. Such a substantial bowl required supports, and these supports in their turn required guy ropes to brace them. These fastenings are called by the same name as the lashings which fix a chariot platform to its chassis. Metaphors relating the structure of the world to a chariot are common: *tian-gai* itself refers to the umbrella over the chariot. The sky is considered as the umbrella on its pole, the earth as the body of the chariot; sometimes the sky is considered as a chariot wheel in a horizontal plane with the Pole Star at its hub. The ancient Chinese chariot had a square body with a circular upper part supported by a single shaft. But although the chariot metaphor implied a central support, it is more common to find that the sky is supported by four or eight pillars, without any attempt to explain how such a system allowed for the revolution of the heavenly bodies.

On the other hand, the obvious discrepancy between the Pole Star as a theoretical centre, which has also to be the centre of the kingdom, itself Zhongguo – the Middle Kingdom – and the actual, off-centre position of this star is explained by the myth of Gong-gong. For when he impaled Mount Buzhou on his horn, the mountain broke and as a result the sky collapsed in the north-west. The heavenly bodies tipped towards the break, while the earth tilted the other way, towards the south-east. And because of this the waters flowed south-eastwards. The name of the mountain means 'Not-Circular'. It seems most likely that this refers both to the breaking of the circle of supporting pillars and to the breaching of whatever retained the waters. For the floods which followed Gong-gong's attack were themselves the subject of a series of myths to which we shall return.

The Separation of Heaven and Earth

In the story of the cosmic egg Pangu's body acts as a link between Heaven and Earth and as a column that keeps them apart. Such a link was, however, a mixed blessing and, according to the *Shu jing*, the order was given to Chongli (or to Chong and Li) to break communications between Heaven and Earth so that there was neither descending nor ascending. The reason for the order is found elsewhere. When Zhuan Hu, Shun, succeeded to Shao Hao, Yao, as emperor, he found that in his predecessor's reign the Nine Li, one of a

number of groups, perverted descendants of the mythical emperor Huang Di, whose excellence lay in troublemaking, had caused confusion between gods and humanity. Since people and gods could occupy the same levels there was no proper order in the sacrifice. Zhuan Hu appointed Chong, governor of the South, to preside over Heaven and to organise the gods in their proper stations, while Li did the same for men as governor of Earth.

The texts seem to be very confused for we also learn the Li was governor of fire, but fire is an element associated with south; Chongli, in fact, was a fire spirit and it is probably the splitting into two which originally led to the confusion. In the *Zuo zhuan* Chong was a younger brother of Shao Hao who became the spirit of wood and, hence, of the east. As such he was Gou Mang who, according to the *Shanhaijing*, had a human head, a bird's body and rode on two dragons. He is said to have had the power to extend the human lifespan on the instructions of the Supreme Being. In the *Zuo zhuan*, Li, as the spirit of fire and of the south, is called Zhurong. The connection with the south ties in with the assertion that 'the princes of Chu are the descendants of Chong and Li'.

The assertion illustrates another role for myth. Chong and Li were, through their descent, linked with the Five Emperors who were themselves ancestral to the ruling Son of Heaven. As the frontiers of the empire expanded, so the rulers of states once on the periphery and now incorporated, whose observance of the *li* and social order was comparable with that of the Chinese, must have descended from Chinese families, otherwise no social order could have been present. As Karlgren explained, discussing such states: 'Their leaders were considered descendants of decadent members of Chinese grandee families', instancing the *chuan* Rong. They lived just to the west of the Zhou and were said by the latter to be descended from the mythical ruler Zhuan Hu, but through his ne'er-do-well son Tao Wu, who was identified with a demon of the same name and a threat to social order.

This was 'a typical example', in Karlgren's words, 'of the workings of the archaic Chinese mind'. But, whatever we may make of these complex stories, two points are noteworthy. Without order, nothing can function: an important element in Chinese religion and ritual is concerned with establishing and maintaining order. As the realm expands therefore, arrangements have to be made to bring the newly incorporated within

the system. Secondly, here are the seeds of the ever-increasing bureaucracy which in the evolving religious systems were to grow into a pantheon organised just like the imperial bureaucracy, with departments to control every aspect and activity of the three divisions of the universe, whether good or bad, approved or disapproved.

Chong and Li may have broken communications between heaven and earth, but these seem to have persisted in various forms though it is not always clear whereabouts heaven was located in relation to the sky. The celestial umbrella continued to be supported by its handle; the central mountain, whether or not it originated from Pangu's stomach, remained; the giant peach tree with its demon gate required a picket to arrest intruding *guei*; and in the *Huainanzi* there is a reference to another tree, the Jian, between the Fu Sang in the east and the Ruo tree in the west which are associated with the sun and the moon. The Jian is the means by which many *di* (here 'spirits') 'descend from above'. The *fei yi* of the Lady Xin Zhui appears to portray her route to Heaven, and Daoist writings make it clear that adepts can make similar journeys. The heavens and human affairs continued to be connected.

The Heavenly Bodies

Chinese myths relating to sun, moon and stars are generally sketchy and inconsistent. Various hypotheses gave an account of the cosmos, as we have seen, but how the heavenly bodies operated depended upon which model one adopted. None was particularly appropriate. A complicating factor was that by the time of the Western Han when texts were being edited and reconstructed, the interest of scholars was mostly in the explanation of irregularities in cosmic order and their correction, rather than in analysis of the physical order.

In view of the acceptance of the relationship between cosmic and human affairs, it followed that if the cosmos could be regulated, then evil could be prevented or averted. For some, Daoists in the main, whose ideas are to be found in the *Huainanzi*, the universe was comparable with the human body. Just as the behaviour and movements of the latter were controlled by the brain and the heart, so the universe was regulated by the *dao*. It was responsible for the movements of the heavenly bodies, the succession of the seasons, the cycles of life and death in plants and animals, the whole systematic pattern of change in the year. Disorder in these, reflected in natural calamities or political disorder, is brought about by human beings. Their superior abilities, despite the fact that they are but one element among the almost numberless created objects, give them the capacity to exert a disproportionate influence on the rest of the cosmos. So long as people control their desire for political power and avoid other excesses, observing the natural order, the *dao* will be preserved and the causes of calamities will not arise.

Another view held, and ascribed to Confucius though it does not seem to relate to what is known of his teaching or to the political theories which were adumbrated in his name, is that the three elements of the cosmos are controlled by *yin* and *yang* in a five-phase system (see page 37). It may be noted in passing that the phase between *yang* and *yin* is one of equilibrium, but *yin* appears to pass directly to *yang* in the next cycle: the maintenance of the pentad seems to be the primary consideration. All three elements interact, but heaven is the ultimate monitoring force which can warn and admonish its son, the emperor, should his behaviour not be consonant with his duty to people and the environment.

Such warnings might take the form of calamities or the appearance of unusual phenomena, the occurance of eclipses, the observing of comets; though not all were inauspicious. The spotting of a dragon or a phoenix, a fall of honeydew might signal heavenly approbation. The need to ensure good relations between the emperor and heaven seems to have been the reason for the institution of the imperial sacrifice to heaven which was maintained from 31 B.C. until A.D. 1915, and a while longer in the Chinese-influenced court of Annam, central Vietnam.

The third model was that implicit in the *I jing*, Book of Changes. Change is normal in the cosmos: even violent phenomena are no more than reflections of a changed situation. In Loewe's words, '. . . there existed one overriding permanent principle. This was nothing less than the fact that change itself was continual, pervasive and unavoidable.' There were the sixty-four hexagrams and the eight trigrams, *ba gua*, two-by-three-line units into which the hexagrams split: these represent heaven/earth, thunder/sun, water/fire, mountain/lake and symbolise the forces which through *yin* and *yang* control nature. Their use enables the professional analyst to study the state of the cosmos, a study which makes it possible to act in such a way as to maintain the system in equilibrium.

Each of the models took into account the whole universe, in which the behaviour of the heavenly bodies was one aspect of the hoped-for

Above. A *bi*, symbol of the circular sky or Heaven. The hole in the centre corresponds to the *lieqiu*, through which the lightning flashes. From Zhou times onwards the *bi* was used in ritual by the king, called the 'Son of Heaven' because provided he remained virtuous Heaven bestowed on him its mandate to rule on earth. This *bi*, decorated with a 'grain pattern', may have been used for the investiture of a prince. Huan ritual object. National Palace Museum, Taipei.

Right. A pair of phoenixes, symbols of happiness and luck and a sign of Heaven's favour. In the time of Zhou, the Phoenix of Mount Qi sang as a happy portent. The phoenix, identified with the empress, was propitious, just as the dragon rain-spirit identified with the emperor was a beneficent creature. Painting on silk, possibly Ming dynasty.

Opposite. Li, the Governor of Fire, riding on a tiger. Also known as Jurong, who presided over the south, he helped to break the link between heaven and earth and thereafter was appointed to keep human beings in their appointed positions in the universal order. Horniman Museum, London.

harmony of the whole. This being so, there was no difficulty in accepting that these bodies played a part in human activities. Aberrations in the behaviour of the one might either lead to, or reflect, aberrations in the behaviour of the other. Records of past celestial anomalies – Chinese observational astronomy seems to have grown from such compilations – compared with human events of the same period and date could enable contemporary celestial phenomena and their influences to be understood. The sun, moon and stars, or, in early times, suns, moons and stars were of great interest, but cosmogonic questions, if asked, do not seem to have found answers, though they remain very much the same from the *Tian wen* 'heavenly questions' of the *Songs of the South*, through the *Huainanzi* to such Tang poets as Liu zongyuan. There does seem to have been a general recognition that there was a time when there was neither heaven nor earth.

There is some evidence to suggest that the Shang believed in the existence of ten suns with whom their ancestors stood in a special relationship, possibly totemic. It seems likely that the Zhou had a single sun. Mencius attributes to Confucius, for whom Zhou was normative, the aphorism: Heaven does not have two suns, the people do not have two kings. But while later Chinese solar astronomy takes no account of a multiplicity of suns, a philosopher in the first century A.D. still found it necessary to refute such a suggestion by scorning the idea that ten suns could sit in a single tree. This somewhat unusual argument depends upon what Allan has called the 'Mulberry Tree tradition'. This is known from literary sources including the *Tian wen*, the *Shanhaijing* and the *Huainanzi*. It may be that the appearance in the *Chu ci* reflects a survival of Shang beliefs in Chu state long after the Zhou with their single sun had come to power.

In the east, to the north of the Black

Tooth Tribe, in the Tang Valley is a pool of hot water. This is where the ten suns bathe. A woman called Xihe, wife of Di Jun, bathes the suns: she is their mother. Above the pool is the *Fu Sang mu* mulberry tree which, though it is 300 *li* high, has leaves like mustard. Nine suns perch in its lower branches: one is on its topmost branch. It is there that the suns go out in turn, one on each day of the ten-day week.

The *Shanhaijing* says that the suns are carried by birds, but the *Huainanzi* declares that the birds are in the suns: these sun birds are sometimes three-legged. In the *Huainanzi*, whose view seems to be supported by Han artists, the sun rides in a chariot drawn by horses, though it sometimes replaces these by dragons. Some say Xihe acts as charioteer, in addition to her other duties as bather, mother and wife of Di Jun. The confusion is compounded by a passage in the *Shanhaijing*, where we are told that the sun has two or three horses near his dwelling: the commentary adds that horses and birds are of similar appearance. In the *Chu ci* the speaker in the poem called *Dong jun*, Lord of the East (The Sun), urges on his horses in line 3; by line 5 he is driving a dragon car. Incidentally, the song concludes, in Hawkes's translation:

Then holding my reins I plunge down to my setting,
On my gloomy night journey back to the East.

There are, in fact, few references to the return journey in the sources.

Di Jun has another wife, Chang Xi, who gave birth to the twelve moons whom she bathes in a pool at the foot of the Ruo tree. This is situated in the far west and is where the sun comes to rest at the end of his diurnal journey. But while the story of the Fu Sang and of Xihe is well-known, that of the Ruo tree and Chang Xi does not seem to have attracted much attention. On the other hand Chang Xi has been identified with Chang-o, otherwise Heng-o, who stole the elixir of immortality from her husband Yi the Archer and fled with it to the moon of which she is sometimes regarded as the goddess. And Yi the Archer is the subject of one of the riddles of the *Tian wen* to which we may now turn: why did the ravens lose their feathers when Yi shot the suns?

An answer to the heavenly question is given by a passage in the *Huainanzi* though it may be earlier. Maspero has suggested that the story was known to Zhou writers. There was a time when children could be left safely in nests, while surplus food grains could be stored at the ends of fields. One might pull the tail of a tiger or of a leopard or tread on a serpent or a snake. Then, in the time of Yao, the ten suns appeared at once, so that grains were withered and grass destroyed and the people had nothing to eat. Yao ordered Archer Yi to shoot at the suns so that nine birds within the suns died, dropping their feathers, and only one sun was left. The appearance of multiple suns reputedly preceded the fall of a dynasty. Some sources say that it led to Yao yielding the imperium to Shun. Again,

Above. Red lacquer panel with the *ba gua* symbols. In the centre are the interlocked *yin* and *yang* symbols, the opposing and complementary principles of the universe. They are surrounded by the Eight Trigrams, the mystic symbols which were the key to knowledge and the basis of calligraphy. Wellcome Institute for the History of Medicine, London.

Above left. An early stone-rubbing showing one of the ten suns crossing the heavens from the hollow mulberry tree, *kong sang* or *fu sang*, in the east, to the ruo tree in the west. The chariot in which the sun is conveyed has the circular canopy over a square chassis which characterised the shape of the Chinese universe.

Opposite. Long dragon surmounted by a medallion showing the white hare of the moon standing at the foot of the cassia tree and pounding the elixir of immortality which Heng-o is to drink, and which will turn her into an immortal toad. Detail from an eighteenth-century embroidered emperor's robe. Victoria and Albert Museum, London.

according to the *Huainanzi* a similar event preceded the fall of Xia, while that of Shang was similarly indicated according to *Bamboo Annals*. The Han writer Wang Chong, who did not believe that heaven could interfere in human affairs, argued that Yi intimidated the suns so that they did not appear together.

The Fu Sang is probably depicted on the *fei yi* from the Han tomb No. 1, while the archer is seen in action on a stone relief from a tomb in Shandong dating from the period A.D. 145-68. The tomb, one of a group of four, seems to link with the story references to Xi Wang Mu, the Queen Mother of the West, and Dong Wang Gong, King Father of the East, whose annual meeting brought *yin* and *yang* together. Now Xi Wang Mu, who is served by birds which are sometimes three-legged, was the one from whom Yi successfully begged the elixir of immortality before it was stolen from him by his wife, Heng-o. She was also

Right. Yao, the fourth of the Five Emperors who taught human beings the arts of civilisation. The sons of the Five Emperors were considered unworthy to inherit the throne. Yao's throne therefore passed to Shun; the upheaval occasioned by this was so violent that all ten suns appeared together and, but for Yi the Good Archer, would have destroyed the world. Painting by Ma Lin. Song dynasty. National Palace Museum, Taipei.

Opposite. Heng-o, goddess of the moon. She was the younger sister of He Bo, Count of the River. When Yi the Divine Archer was sent by Yao to stop the river flooding in Gaoliang, he shot and injured the spirit responsible for the flooding, but spared Heng-o who accompanied him, aiming an arrow to lodge in her hair. In gratitude, Heng-o became his wife. Modern terracotta. Musée Guimet, Paris.

Below. Yi arriving on his twice-monthly visit to the moon, where his wife Heng-o lived in the Palace of Great Cold which he built out of cinnamon trees. Though Heng-o had stolen the pill of immortality, Yi too obtained immortality, but had to live separately, in the Palace of the Sun or Palace of the Lonely Park. Heng-o represented the cold, female principle of *yin*, whereas Yi represented the warm, male principle of *yang*. Korean mirror, A.D. 936–1392. Seligman Collection.

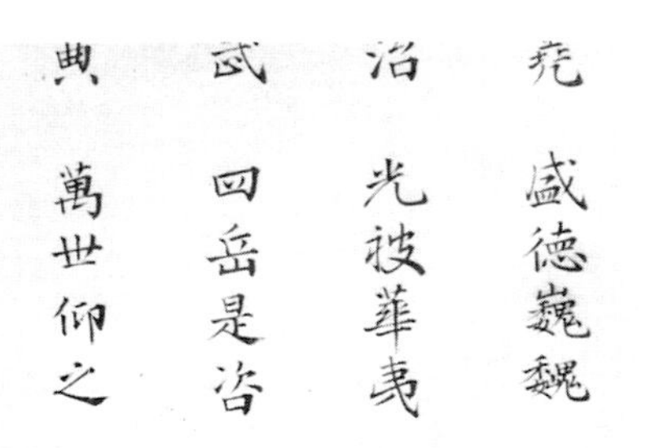

associated with the west and fled to the moon where she became a toad (see page 62). There is certainly nothing in this tradition to suggest she is also the mother of the moon.

Incidentally there is never any clear indication of the paternity of either sun or moon, nor is there any other account of their creation. Indeed, once the primal vapour *yuanqi* had come into being they seem, as *yang* and *yin*, to have a creative role of their own. *Qi*, which I have called vapour, is translated as 'pneuma' by Schafer, giving a sense of its spiritual implication. In a passage which Loewe quotes from the *Huainanzi*:

Heaven has set out the Sun and the Moon and arrayed the constellations; it has regulated Yin and Yang and it has stretched out the four seasons. . .

There is nothing here of the origin of the *er jing*, the two luminosities, to say nothing of the stars. They exist: Heaven arranges them. To create is not to make *ab initio* but to alter from one state to another. In a different passage, it seems that fiery *qi* forms a hot essence which may be the sun, or its basic raw material; chill *qi* relates to the moon in a similar way.

What remains from these processes, if that term is not too positive, constitutes the stars, which are presumably both *yin* and *yang*. The ideogram *xing*, star, according to another Han text, is formed by placing *ri*, sun, above *sheng*, which can mean to beget, to bring forth, to produce or even to be born. Although the earliest form of *sheng* shows a squatting woman with an emergent child, we are probably only justified in concluding with Schafer that stars are 'sun-generated', but since the sun is so indisputably male/*yang*, we may wonder what has happened to the moon *qi*. But, whatever their origins,

the stars play a continuous role in the affairs of the universe whether as single stars, asterisms or constellations and either are, or are inhabited by, beings who are male or female. There is also a Daoist belief that when these males and females are visiting earth, as they do, the relevant points in the sky are dark. Finally we should note that not only the names but also the groupings together are almost wholly different from those familiar in western Eurasiatic astronomy and astrology.

Of all the myths which centre about the stars there is one that may parallel, indeed be linked with, the annual meeting of Xi Wang Mu, who among other things seems to have controlled the constellations, and Dong Wang Gong. The myth concerns Zhi nu, the Weaver Maid, who is also called *Tian sun* grand-daughter of heaven, and Qian niu, the Oxherd (who are respectively Vega in the constellation Lyra, and Altair in Aquila). The Han astronomer Zhang Heng describes them as standing to the right and left of the Starry River, the Celestial Han, the Milky Way. Weaver Maid toiled year after year at her loom weaving the cloth of heaven with its pattern of clouds. The god of heaven arranged her marriage with the Oxherd who lived on the west bank of the Celestial Han.

Unfortunately, in the pleasure of marriage the weaving was neglected and Zhi nu, who in one version was the daughter of the god of heaven, was ordered back to her loom. Now

Right. Shoulao, the god of longevity, who was at first a stellar deity, the Old Man of the South Pole, under whose influence the nation enjoyed peace. He is characterised by his large bald head and the peach, symbol of long life, which he carries. Wellcome Institute for the History of Medicine, London.

Opposite. Jade screen illustrating the art of weaving silk. Sericulture was one of the basic arts of Chinese civilisation taught by the serpent-bodied Fuxi, the first of the mythical Three Sovereigns. The Heavenly Weaver-girl was the grand-daughter of Heaven. Jade screen, reign of Kang Xi (1662-1722). Seattle Art Museum, Washington.

One of the many star-gods who in later times were considered to be functionaries in the bureaucracy of the Supreme Emperor. Handscroll, attributed to Liang Linzan. Tang dynasty. Osaka Municipal Museum of Fine Arts.

it is only on the seventh night of the seventh month that the couple are allowed to meet when she crosses the river on a bridge of birds.

Now, in the middle of her pleasure,
the wretched waterclock speeds on;
After they have parted, she resents the
eternity of Heaven.

Some say that her original punishment limited her visits to every seventh night but that the messenger crow made a mistake in the message. Another tale says that she was Xi Wang Mu's grand-daughter who, while on earth, fell in love with an Oxherd and was brought back to Heaven. There her grandmother drew a line, with a hairpin, which became the celestial river and separated the lovers. Perhaps her grandmother really used the *sheng*, the ornament which she wears in her chignon and represents a weaver's shuttle.

Heaven's grandchild was sometimes considered 'the quintessence of *yin* which flowed from the moon toad' and one lucky mortal Kuo Han had a love affair with her, which the lovers celebrated in alternate verses, a tradition to which we shall return. But a poem from Dun-huang which has been translated by Waley indicates her most important role so far as human beings are concerned. Brides came under her special care, as did the arts of spinning, weaving and embroidery. On the seventh night of the seventh month girls 'begged for skill' and held competitions in needlework and the threading of needles. Offerings of seasonal fruits were made with wine and sweetmeats.

It was hoped that the Maid herself would honour the occasion in the form of a spider and weave a web across an opened gourd. The ladies of the Tang emperor Xuan Zong used, we are told, on this night to shut a spider in a box. In the morning the tension of the web which the spider had woven was inspected and the tightness or otherwise of the weave was taken as a judgment on the weaving skill of its captor.

But the Weaver Maid herself might be captured as a bride. In the *Huainanzi* we learn that the fulfilled Daoist adept knows how to bestride Fei-lian, a wind-god and caster of dynastic cauldrons for the Xia; to follow Dun-yu, a mythical tiger; to light up the ten suns; to take, as his messenger, the Count of the Wind and, as his vassal, the Spirit of Thunder; Kuafu will be his braggart; his junior wife will be the goddess of the Lo River; for consort he will have the Weaver Maid.

Kuafu, a son of Gong-gong, overestimated his ability and challenged the very sun whom he overtook in the valley where he sets. In his thirst he drank both the Yellow and the Wei rivers, but their waters were not enough. He turned north towards the Great Marsh, which was the home of the two daughters of the Emperor Shun, but died of thirst before he reached it.

The goddess of the River Lo was Fufei. Some say that she was a daughter of Fuxi, others that, like Nugua, she was his sister. However this may be, she was a most desirable lady who passed 'each day in idle, wanton pleasures' and was sought by the shaman hero of the *Li sao*, but, 'all wills and caprices, she was hard to woo'. She was also the wife of the god of the Yellow River who had been shot by Yi the Archer with whom she subsequently lived – Hawkes suggests 'as conqueror's spoils' – on Mount Qiongshi. And here, but for the Weaver Maid, we have come full circle, for other sources say that when Yi shot the god of the river he spared his younger sister whose name was Heng-o. She, in gratitude, married him and became the goddess of the moon.

Earth, Water and Air

We have been looking at the cosmos and at some of the ways in which its parts were believed to interact as well as at the means by which it was hoped that such interactions could be rendered if not beneficial, at least neutral: the problems of balance on a cosmic scale. It is now time to consider interactions at a lower level and how rivers, winds, mountains, and seas were thought of on a less theoretical plane.

Earth consisted of a square with four mountains at the cardinal points and a fifth at the centre. There were four rivers, of different colours, which flowed outwards from the centre to the four edges of the earth, apparently unobstructed by the cardinal mountains: the point does not arise. For some Chinese at least the eastern sea was a reality: those of the other directions were a construct which symmetry required, though Yu, among whose scientific inventions was geography, is said to have travelled to the four seas. On these occasions he held meetings of the feudatories beyond the empire. To visit the four mountains was part of the ritual by which the emperor took possession of his realm. Sacrifices to the rivers were another element in the system. According to Confucius, the influence of the mountains and the rivers, the gods of the earth and of the harvest were sufficient to control the world. Many traditions are concerned with these matters; that they are often contradictory or obscure is unsurprising, given the size of the area from which they are drawn and the three and half millennia of writings in which they have been recorded.

As we have seen, one of the results of Gong-gong's attack on Mount Bu-zhou was that all the waters flowed south-eastwards: so much for symmetry. The arrival of the water in the eastern sea created no problem, for there was a bottomless hole into which flowed not only all the rain and the rivers and the sea itself, but also the waters of the Celestial Han, the Milky Way. Nearby were the Islands of the Immortals, so real that Qin Shi Huang Di and others sent ships in search of them. One of the difficulties for the seachers was that the islands floated freely at first, until the immortals, annoyed by their collisions with other lands, persuaded the Ruler of Heaven to anchor their paradise. The latter was sympathetic and ordered Yuqiang to fix the islands in position.

This he did by employing giant tortoises in teams of three to take it in turns, each period of duty lasting 60,000 years, to hold the islands in place. According to the *Liezi* Nugua cut off the feet of a tortoise to fix in place the cardinal points: in Indian tradition it is a tortoise which supports the churn-stick, Mount Mandora, when the gods and demons churn the ocean. Yuqiang's plan worked well until one day some giants, on a fishing trip, caught some of the tortoises and two of the islands drifted northwards and sank. The emperor of heaven, angered by the episode, reduced all giants in size: they had walked to the islands. The remaining three islands continued as an abode for immortals; the best known was Penglai which is said to be vase-shaped.

Shang Chitan has suggested that the lower section of the *fei yi* from Mawangdui (see page 39) is a picture of Penglai, the entwined dragons forming a *hu* vase whose base, a white slab perhaps of jade, is supported by a straining figure, Yuqiang, who is flanked by a pair of tortoises and stands on a couple of coiled fish. The illustration does not accord with the texts, but there is a considerable degree of support for the idea that the theme is that of Penglai. It has also been suggested, by some scholars, that the bat-like creature which hovers above the vase, between the dragon heads but under the topmost white slab which supports a trident-like motif and two birds with long tails, is Fei-lian. The birds would be read as a pair of phoenixes, often a symbol of conjugal happiness, but here perhaps heavenly messengers.

According to the *Shanhaijing* Yuqiang has a bird's body and a human face: green serpents hang from his ears, red serpents are under his feet. (In the *fei yi* the caryatid figure has a red snake passing between his legs: the snake is tied to his left leg.) He is thought to live at the extreme limits of the world to the north, where he was visited by Yu the Great; he is associated with the north-west wind. As a spirit linked with the sea he has the form of a great whale, *gun*, with human hands and feet and rides upon a pair of dragons. The *gun* can turn into a giant bird, *peng*, whose wings, when it rises from the water, make great waves. As it flies south for six months the spread of its wings darkens the sky: then it comes to rest in the southern sea. This seems to be a legendary model for the monsoon wind pattern of the China Sea.

According to Zhuangzi the *peng* is the *gun* in another form, several thousand *li* broad and of unknown length, whose back is like Tai Shan and whose wings resemble the clouds around the sky. When it moves south, it flaps its wings on the water for 3000 *li*, then mounting on a whirlwind like the whorls of a goat's horn for 90,000 *li* 'till far removed from the cloudy vapours it bears on its back the blue sky, and then it shapes its course for the South and proceeds to the ocean there'. According to Zhuangzi a quail by the side of a marsh laughed at it and said: 'Where is it going to? I spring up with a bound and come down again when I have reached but a few fathoms, and then fly around among the brushwood and bushes: this is the perfection of flying. Where is that creature going to?' In Zhuangzi's view, this shows the difference between the small and the great.

In later Chinese sources the *peng* is a creature of the African coast in the region of Zanzibar. According to a writer on twelfth- to thirteenth-

century trade the bird was so vast that, as it rose into the sky, it momentarily obscured the sun. It could swallow a camel; its quills were big enough to serve as water containers. The *peng* has here been conflated with the 'roc' of which Marco Polo wrote that it was big enough to swallow an elephant. The linking of a whale with a bird is unexpected, but it is probably relevant to note that in the *Huainanzi* we learn that a broom-star comet appears when a whale dies, though the apparent explanation that the whale is a *yin* creature and as such is born from the water cannot be said to advance the argument to any great extent.

Yuqiang, who is referred to in the *Chu ci* as Boqiang (it calls him a wind star, asking rather plaintively 'where does the warm wind live?'), was only one of a number of winds associated with the eight cardinal points, the gates of the world, and with the trigrams; each represented a magic power. There was, in addition, a Count of the Wind, Feng Bo, who was also known as Fei-lian. In a text of the fourth century A.D. he is described as having a body like a stag, a head like a sparrow, a serpent's tail, horns and the markings of a panther.

Opposite left. The lower part of the universe, showing the animals and elements of the four cardinal directions surrounding the square earth, which is lapped on all four sides by the primeval ocean in which it floats. Bronze marriage mirror of the Tang dynasty, probably early eighth century A.D. Seattle Art Museum, Washington. Eugene Fuller Memorial Collection.

Centre. The Black Warrior – tortoise and serpent – which symbolises the north. Unlike the other directions, the north was never worshipped in early times, and was feared as the home of the destructive god of the ocean wind. But the Han ruled under the protection of water and of the north and sacrificed to the Black Emperor. White slip on earthenware, Northern Wei (A.D. 385-535). Seattle Art Museum, Washington. Eugene Fuller Memorial Collection.

Left. Yuqiang, god of the ocean wind, listening to the Doctrine. Painting by Zhao Bozhu of the Song dynasty; he belonged to the 'northern' school of painting, long associated with a sect of Zen Buddhism, and the subject shows a preoccupation with the new faith in relation to the old deity. National Palace Museum, Taipei.

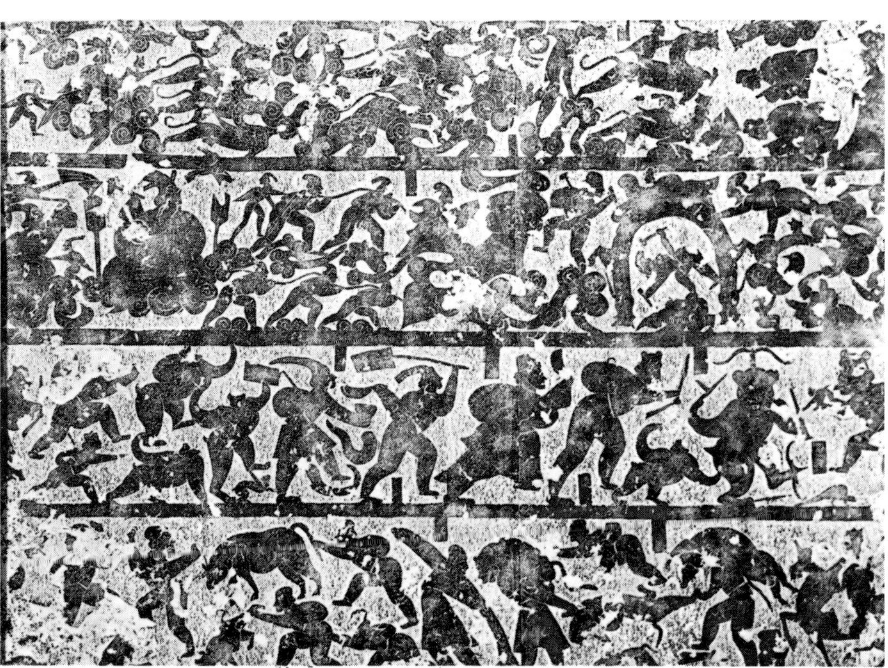

Below. The Thunderer, an ancient storm-deity, seen routing men and beasts with the sound of thunder, which he produces by beating drums with a hammer. His chariot is drawn by six boys. In later times, like Feng Bo, he became an official in the Ministry of Thunder, and was called Lei Gong, Duke of Thunder. Rubbing of a stone relief from the tomb of the Wu family in Shandong, Han dynasty. Národní Galerie, Prague.

On the other hand Sima Qian knew him as a historical personage famed for his marching and buried on a mountain in the west of the empire.

On the east on Tai Shan, great mountain, was a creature called Fei which resembled a white-headed, one-eyed bull with a serpent tail: according to the *Shanhaijing*, if it waded in a river, it dried up; as it grazed the grass died; it brought pestilence to the realm. Wang Ch'ung described how it shrivels and burns the branches and leaves of trees because it is essentially *yang*. The winds are in a great sack from whose mouth the Count may direct them in what direction he wills.

Fei-lian supported Chiyu in his struggle for power with Huang Di for the succession to the Three Sovereigns. (He is remembered in this context because when Liu Bang opened the campaign which ended in the installation of the Han dynasty, he sacrificed to Huang Di, made offerings to Chiyu and annointed his drums with blood.) We shall return to this struggle below (see page 96). Here it is sufficient to note that in the *Shanhaijing* the Ying Dragon brought the waters to the aid of Huang Di. Chiyu called on the Count of the Wind and the Master of the Rain, who provided their phenomena in abundance. Huang Di invoked the descent of a daughter of Heaven whose name was Ba, Drought, so that the rain stopped and Huang Di was able to kill Chiyu. Fei-lian was punished for his support but took his revenge by creating storms in the south.

Huang Di's successor Yao sent the Archer Yi to restore order. The latter ordered the people to place a great sheet anchored with stones in front of their houses to divert the wind so that he might ride to the top of the mountain where the Count lived. He saw the wind in the shape of a great sack of yellow and white material which heaved in and out gustily. He shot an arrow at it, whereupon the monster took refuge in a deep cave with sword drawn. The latter fired again and wounded Fei-lian in the knee, forcing his surrender. Thereafter the winds were properly controlled.

Feng Bo sometimes appears as an old man with a white beard, red and blue cap and yellow cloak. Others say that the winds are managed by an old woman Feng Popo, who can be seen riding on her tiger amid the clouds.

The Master of the Rain

During the reign of Shennong, Chi Songzi, who had taught his sovereign to walk through fire protected by liquid jade, saved the realm from a fearful drought. He ordered water to be poured into an earthenware bowl. Then he took a branch from a mountainside tree and, dipping it in the water, sprinkled the earth. Clouds gathered at once and the rain poured upon the earth until the rivers overflowed their banks. As a reward he

was made Master of the Rain and given a dwelling place on Mount Kunlun (see page 76).

Other methods of drought-breaking were more drastic. Tang offered himself as a sacrificial victim (see page 21). A prince of Lu wished to expose to the sun an emaciated sorceress, but was dissuaded on the grounds that it would only make matters worse. Emaciation turns the face upwards to heaven and heaven will not let the rain fall on such people lest the water enter their nostrils. Han Wudi was told that if he were to boil a counsellor it would rain.

Chi Songzi was also thought to have the form of a silkworm chrysalis with a blackfaced concubine who had a serpent in each hand and a red and a green serpent in her right and left ear. His other companion was a one-legged bird *shang yang*. Such a bird once appeared at the court of Chi where it descended from the palace roof to alight in the reception courtyard. There it spread its wings and danced upon its single leg. The prince of Chi sent an embassy to Lu to enquire from Confucius what such a visit portended. The sage recognised its significance at once. Such an appearance foretold rain. As he explained:

In former times young boys used to fold one leg and shrug their shoulders, singing:
Heaven will cause rain to fall abundantly;
The shang yang *beats its drum and dances.*

Now that the bird was in Chi, heavy rain would unquestionably fall. Ditches should be dug and dykes repaired, lest all the land should be inundated. The prince of Chi took the advice of the sage and his realm escaped without damage, but the rest of the land, including Lu, suffered greatly. Confucius held no official position in his home state.

Above. Tai Shan, the mountain of the east from which the sun began its daily journey and to which in early times the souls of the dead were thought to return. The most important dynastic sacrifices were performed on its almost inaccessible peak. Landscape engraving from the *Ming-han ming-shan tu-ban huaji*. Ming dynasty. University of Hong Kong.

Opposite. One of the three islands of the Immortals in the Eastern Sea. The inhabitants of this eastern paradise not only had the secret of immortality, but also the alchemical secrets of making gold. People and animals on the islands were all coloured white, while all the buildings were made of silver and gold. People could not approach the islands, for their ships were driven back by storms. Painting by Wang Zhen, Song dynasty. National Palace Museum, Taipei.

The Cardinal Mountains

At the edges of the square earth, on the cardinal axes, there were four mountains. Two we have already met in connnection with the sun's journey across the sky. A third marked the sun's zenith in the southern sky. The fourth was far to the north, always a dangerous region. Logic and the pentad system added a fifth which seems, as we have seen, to be a kind of *axis mundi*. This pattern was reflected in the lay-out of the city and its gates. When the emperor succeeded to the throne he took possession of the realm by visiting four mountains. At court an official, or officials, called Four Mountains represented the outlying vassals. Of the original four, one, Tai Shan, seems to have remained a focus of cult, but in the west, another mountain, Kunlun, took the place of the sun's evening halting place and it together with Tai Shan became the centre of a series of beliefs which steadily increased in importance in Han times.

Tai Shan

The physical Tai Shan is situated in Shandong and seems to have been considered an especially sacred site long before Qin Shi Huang Di incorporated its cult into the imperial ritual, a pattern which was to be followed and reinforced by his Han successors. When Duke Huan of Chi was making a bid for the hegemony in the seventh century B.C. he is said by Sima Qian to have offered the *feng* sacrifice on the mountain, thus implying that the imperial mountain was a part of his fief but his virtue was insufficient and the tribute from the distant regions did not arrive. On the other hand, when Han Wudi made his sacrifice *feng-shan* in 110 B.C., a *de xing* (a 'star of virtue', *de* being, above all, royal virtue) shone in the heavens. Later, in Tang times, when Li Shimin was on his way to the mountain to make the sacrifice, a comet was seen in that part of the sky called *Tai wei gong* and the imperial progress was halted in the vicinity of Luoyang, the ceremony abandoned and, as a further precaution, the imperial diet was reduced.

For some Tai Shan was the location of the mulberry tree from which the sun set out each day in his journey across the sky. For Daoists the mountain was an abode of the immortals.

Loewe translates an inscription from the back of a bronze mirror, itself a cosmic symbol:

If you climb Mount Tai, you may see the immortal beings. They feed on the purest jade, they drink from the springs of manna. They yoke the scaly dragons to their carriages, they mount the floating clouds. The white tiger leads them . . . they ascend straight to heaven. May you receive a never-ending span, long life that lasts for 1000 years with a fit place in office and safety for your children and grandchildren.

It seems that the entrance to the *huang quan* (Yellow Springs), that realm beneath the earth where the souls of those who did not achieve union with the immortals were thought to continue in a somewhat joyless version of life on earth, was located near Tai Shan. This too added to its numinous nature. Yet, it is noteworthy that there appears to have been considerable uncertainty about the rites proper to an imperial ceremony on the mountain when Han Wudi wished to undertake such an event. One explanation may be that the Confucian scholars were reluctant to encourage a ritual that did not offer them full control. Whatever the reason, the emperor, when he resolved to offer the sacrifices *feng* and *shan*, turned to the local shamans for advice on the procedures to be followed. They would, in any event, seem likely repositories for what was originally and in essence a local ritual.

The intention of the act was to

Centre. The Five Holy Mountains – those of the four cardinal directions together with the Mountain of the Centre. The five mountains were associated with the five elements and thus with the whole mystical system of the Chinese and, as a group, played a central part in dynastic ritual. Yu was said to have discovered that the four cardinal mountains were laid out in an exact square. National Palace Museum, Taipei.

Opposite left. The five cardinal points represented by their emblematic figures in hunting and battle scenes. The Five Mountains were the source of power (thus the dynastic swords were made from ores collected from them and swords were hidden in the mountains), and blood sacrifice upheld their power. Pottery tile of the Han dynasty. Musée Cernuschi, Paris.

Below. The growth of Daoism in the Later Han period led to an increase in the representation of Daoist deities and the various Daoist paradises. Xi Wang Mu and Dong Wang Gong were depicted on the backs of mirrors and on tombs. Models of the mountains on which the celestial palaces were believed to be found were made in pottery and, occasionally, in bronze. Elaborate miniature gardens were also constructed to serve as evocations of the paradises of the immortals. Shaoxing, where this proto-Yue ware vessel was excavated, was an important centre of popular Daoism. Western Jin dynasty (A.D. 265-316).

legitimize the possession of territory, a fact that lends colour to the view that the spirit of a territory resides in its central mountain or in its surrogate, the phallic symbol of the soil-deity. It is interesting, therefore, to note that in 119 B.C., before Han Wudi made his ascent of Tai Shan, his general Ho Juping celebrated the conquest of eighty barbarian chiefs by the ascents of Langgusu and Huyan to make *feng* and *shan* sacrifices whose intention seems to have been the validation of his title to the erstwhile barbarian territories.

Such a ritual performed by the emperor himself was not, however, to be undertaken lightly, for the commentators implied that Shi Huang Di had died prematurely after his failure to complete the sacrifices once he had ascended the mountain: winds had driven him from the summit. He had been rejected by heaven, though it should be noted that it was ten years after the aborted ceremony before the rejection took place. Only a sage of supreme merit could carry out such a ritual.

The emperor Wudi set out upon a progress to inspect the east (visitation of the regions had been instituted by Huang Di himself) and to make the sacrifice as the result of the discovery of an antique bronze tripod by a shaman which he claimed had been associated with the Yellow Emperor. Since the latter made the sacrifices on Tai Shan, and subsequently joined the immortals in heaven, Wudi, by following a similar course of action, would achieve the same end. In recognition of Huang Di's precedence, Wudi sacrificed at his tomb, though he is reported to have been disconcerted at the existence of a tomb to one who had gone directly to heaven. He was reassured on learning that it sheltered his robes which had remained on earth.

He then established a group to support the cult of Tai Shan and forbad the felling of timber on the mountain. Next he carried out the *feng* sacrifice on a large, specially constructed mound. What took place was recorded secretly on tablets of jade. He made a second *feng* sacrifice and followed this next day with a *shan* sacrifice at the north-east corner of the foot of Tai Shan, appropriate to a deity of the soil. The year 110 B.C. was designated *yuan feng* ('Primal Feng').

Mount Kunlun

There were those for whom the *Fu Sang mu*, from which the sun began its daily journey, was situated on Tai Shan. The *Ruo mu*, on which it came to rest, was less precisely located but it was, according to the *Huainanzi*, west of the *Jian mu* which, as we have seen, served as a passage for spirits to reach earth from above. It was an *axis mundi*, though neither it nor the Ruo tree was stated to be on a mountain, nor was either the focus of a developed cult.

The Tang poet Yang Jiong, who was interested in astronomy, speaks of the sun at *Ruo mu* shining upon Kunlun. And Kunlun was the mountain in the far west which became the reciprocal of the far east's Tai Shan. But while modern cartographers show the Kunlun range on the boundary between Xinjiang and Xijang (Tibet), 82°-87° E, 36°N, the Kunlun of the mythographers moved further west the further the Chinese penetrated into central Asia. When Indian cosmographic ideas became familiar to Chinese scholars, largely as a result of the introduction of Buddhism, Kunlun was identified with Sumeru, though the latter's centrality, in contrast with the peripheral location of the former, made such an identification inappropriate.

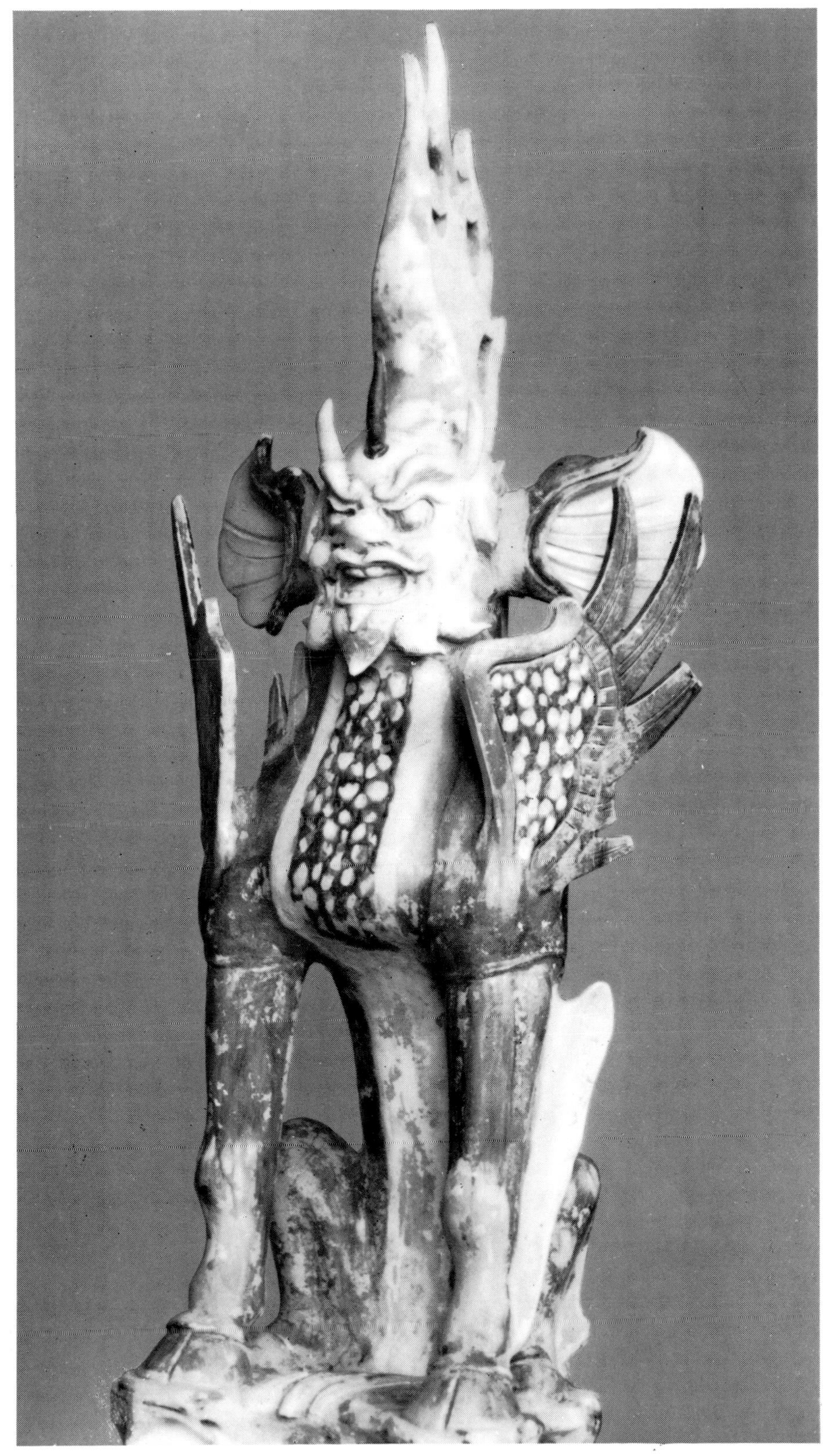

The *Shanhaijing* asserts that the Ruo River encircles the heights of Kunlun, a statement which may link the mountain and the sun's western perch, but it does not imply that it, like the *Jian mu*, was an *axis mundi* as Sumeru unquestionably was. Yet the character *shan* (mountain) implies three peaks and Loewe has pointed out that Xi Wang Mu, Queen Mother of the West, and her eastern counterpart are shown on the central one of three pillars at the tombs at Yi-nan as though each was occupying an axis in a three-peak system: *Fu Sang mu*, *Jian mu* and *Ruo mu* from east to west. We should note in passing the widespread equivalence of tree and mountain as cosmic symbols, characteristically expressed in Javanese where the central motif of the shadow theatre is known both as *gunungan* (mountain) and *kekayon* (tree).

Left. Figure of a supernatural creature with monster head, elephant's ears, wings and cloven hooves – the sort of hybrid animal which was supposed to guard the entrances to Kunlun. Such figures were placed in tombs to guard them, or perhaps to lead the soul to the Kunlun paradise. Glazed earthenware, Tang dynasty. Victoria and Albert Museum, London.

Opposite left. The lid of a *hun-ping* or urn of the soul, a type of ritual vessel modelled in the shape of a fairy mountain with subsidiary peaks and designed to emit the vapours exhaled by all living nature. The summit is square, like the earth, while the base is lapped by waters. Kunlun was conceived of as such a mountain. Yue ware, porcelain, third century A.D. Cleveland Museum of Art, Ohio. Purchase, Leonard C. Hannä, Jr. Bequest.

Opposite right. The Western Paradise of Kunlun as depicted on a Buddhist scroll. Buddha sits enthroned and surrounded by his court of celestial beings. Indian influence led to the identification of Kunlun with the Indian Sumeru, so that this Buddhist paradise is surrounded by waters, which gave immortality. Religionskundliche Sammlung der Universitäts, Marburg.

The origin of the name of the far western mountain is obscure. In the geographical section, known as the Tribute of Yu, of the *Shu jing* there is an account of a region with three rivers: the Yellow River flows eastwards, the Black River southwards while the third flows west into the Shifting Sands. (Sumeru is the source of four rivers flowing towards the cardinal points.) In the vicinity of the Shifting Sands are the Rong tribes (see page 59) amongst whom are included the Kunlun. The term, used to describe an ethnic group, continues in Chinese and is applied to people in south-east Asia who have black skins and frizzy hair, sometimes mythical (they ride elephants underwater to harvest pearls), sometimes meaning negritos of that region. From the latter comes its application to African negroes when these first became known to the Chinese in Tang times as a few black slaves reached China.

There is nothing to connect the Kunlun with a mountain, indeed they are located in the region of the Shifting Sands; but the name was transferred both to the very real mountains on the route between India and Burma and a well-known source of jade, as well as to a sacred peak encircled by the Ruo River which was inhabited by spirits whose white tiger bodies were topped with human faces. Its governor, Jianwu, was distinguished by his nine-tailed body. His attendants were a bee-like bird whose bite or sting killed cattle and shrivelled trees (a parallel perhaps to

Right. Li Tieguai, one of the Eight Immortals of Daoism, who lived in the Yuan (Mongol) dynasty but was said to have received instruction from Laozi. He had magical powers and the gourd he carried contained medicines to revive the dead. Porcelain figure, *c.* nineteenth century. Wellcome Institute for the History of Medicine, London.

Opposite left. A fairy walking on the waves. In Chinese Buddhism much emphasis was placed on fairies, who inhabited mountains and water. They were often linked with the Immortals and imagined on every peak, but especially on Kunlun. Painting after Qian Xuan of the Yuan dynasty (thirteenth century). British Museum, London.

Below. Temple of the Lamas in Beijing. Buddhism came to China from many sources, but the forms it adopted allowed it to become closely linked with Daoism. Mongol rulers encouraged Lamaism because of its magical practices.

the way in which drought was caused by Fei of Tai Shan), and a man-eating creature like a ram with four horns, called Tulou.

Nearby was an all-consuming Mountain of Fire, while on Kunlun itself was a cavern where, according to the *Shanhaijing*, 'there is a person who wears a *sheng* on her head with a tiger's teeth and a leopard's tail. . .' The person is Xi Wang Mu, Queen Mother of the West. Other sources say that she occupies the Yao peak of Kunlun where she receives and entertains her visitors, among whom was the Archer Yi. He obtained from her the elixir of immortality, later stolen by his wife (see page 65).

Xi Wang Mu

The Shang knew a Xi Mu, probably Western Mother, to whom offerings were made. Nothing is known of her role or cult. Much later she appears, if indeed it is the same deity, as one of a number of creators and innovators. Others are Fuxi and Huang Di, who are a primal part of human history. Her cult, though she is mentioned as a source of the elixir of immortality in the second century B.C., did not become important until the later Han period: she was closely associated with Daoism. When Laozi died, he departed towards the west on the back of a buffalo bound for her paradise which was the western equivalent of Penglai. The peaches from her garden also conferred immortality. She travelled on the back of a crane or of a phoenix and is frequently thus depicted on popular prints. She was also the goddess of plagues and epidemics.

For the Daoists she is the primal breath *yuanqi* of Tai Yin. At a mundane level she lives in a nine-tiered metal city on the summit of Kunlun, while in the heavens she lives on the Flowery Platform under the Pole Star. She inhabits the right eye of man while Dong Wang Gong inhabits his left: they also have palaces under the right and the left nipple respectively. She is served by Jade Girls who act as her messengers, as do the three green birds. They are three-legged like the birds in the suns, according to some sources, who bring her food. In one of the stories of the birth of Laoze we learn that Xuan miao yu nu ('Esoteric miracle jade woman') dreamed that she swallowed a meteor. Eighty-one years later she gave birth to the sage who was thus linked, from the first, with Xi Wang Mu in the mythical canon of Daoism.

At her court on Kunlun Xi Wang Mu entertained Mu, king of Zhou, who travelled there with his eight chargers, *ba jun*, who became symbols of imperial journeying and were featured in paintings as late as the Tang dynasty. According to the *Mu tianzi chuan* (Tale of Mu, Son of Heaven), the king gave her a return

banquet on the shores of lake Yao which lay near her palace. So overwhelmed was he by the delights of the western paradise that he failed to return home. In the *Liezi* he is made to observe:

Alas! I who am a king have neglected virtue for pleasure. Will not future generations look back and criticise me for my errors?

But not all visitors were so impressed. A poet writing about 125 B.C., for whom Xi Wang Mu dwelt in a cave, remarks:

If one has to live such a life and never die, to survive for ten thousand generations will not be a source of joy.

Traditionally Xi Wang Mu descended from Kunlun to visit Han Wudi, whose preoccupation with immortality we have already noted. The visit took place on the seventh day of the seventh month, the very day when the Weaver Maid and the Oxherd enjoy their annual conjunction. This union, like the annual meeting of Xi Wang Mu and Dong Wang Gong, with whom perhaps Han Wudi was to be equated after the rites on Tai Shan, symbolised the unity of *yin* and *yang*. The dragon and the tiger which appear together on the throne of Xi Wang Mu are also *yin-yang*.

The elixir is pounded at her behest for those whom she deems fit recipients. But she is also the guardian of the magic peaches which grow in the gardens within the golden ramparts of her palace on the shores of the Lake of Gems. The tree is in leaf every three thousand years: its fruit takes three thousand years to ripen. Then it is Xi Wang Mu's birthday and all the immortals come to her feast by her magic fountain. There they enjoy paws of bear, lips of monkey, livers of dragon and the peaches which give immortality. It was the dishes that made up this feast which were stolen by Monkey (see page 128).

Smiths and the Dynastic Mountains

Perhaps the best-known sacrifices to effect some special operation are those which concern sword-making. A series of texts recounts the forging of magic swords, usually to serve as dynastic palladia. These seem to have originated in the region about the mouth of the Yangtze, in the kingdoms of Wu and Yue. It is possible that they were originally Indonesian stories, at the time when the coastal strip was inhabited by Indonesian-speaking peoples, for there are traces of similar stories in somewhat etiolated form to be found in medieval Javanese dynastic histories.

A basic version of the story is given in the *Wu Yue Chunqiu*. This tells how Ho Liu, king of Wu, commissioned a pair of swords from the smith Gan Jiang and his wife Mo Ye. They set out to the Five Mountains to collect suitable ores and then, at an auspicious moment, began the work of making the swords. But at the end of three months the metal had still not been extracted from the ore: the essence of the iron would not melt and flow. Mo Ye asked her husband why this was. He replied that he did not understand the principle, though he remembered that in similar circumstances his master and the latter's wife had cast themselves into the furnace in order that the work should be

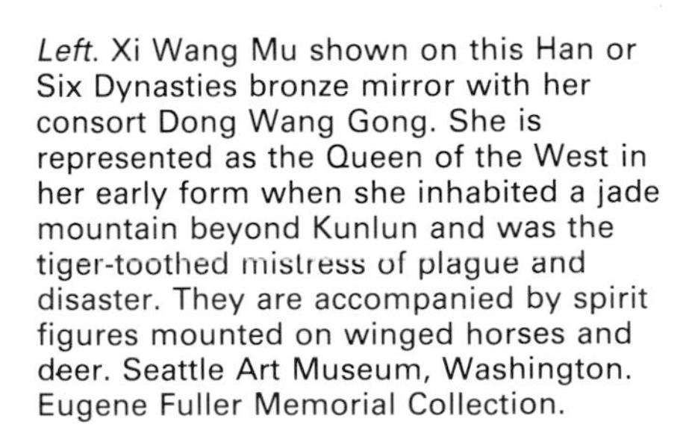

Left. Xi Wang Mu shown on this Han or Six Dynasties bronze mirror with her consort Dong Wang Gong. She is represented as the Queen of the West in her early form when she inhabited a jade mountain beyond Kunlun and was the tiger-toothed mistress of plague and disaster. They are accompanied by spirit figures mounted on winged horses and deer. Seattle Art Museum, Washington. Eugene Fuller Memorial Collection.

Opposite. The spirts of the blessed gathering outside the golden ramparts of Xi Wang Mu's palace on Kunlun, which can be seen emerging from the clouds. All who approach the court of the Royal Mother of the Western Paradise hope to partake of the fruits of immortality. Anonymous painting, eighteenth century. British Museum, London.

accomplished. Then Mo Ye threw her nail-parings and hair-clippings into the furnace and, after the bellows had been reapplied and more fuel added to the furnace, the swords were successfully made. The male sword was called Gan Jiang, the female Mo Ye. The smith hid the male sword and gave the female one to the king. On testing the sword, the latter realised that he had been cheated and in his wrath he killed the smith. Gan Jiang, as he died, told his pregnant wife that his death would be avenged by their unborn son and disclosed to her the hiding place of the male sword.

When the son was old enough, his mother told him the story and he went to seek the sword. Having found it, he used it to decapitate himself. A stranger then appeared and took both the sword and the head of Gan Jiang's son to the king, who threw the head into a cauldron in order to melt it. When it failed to melt, the stranger persuaded the king to allow his own head to be cut off in order that it, by falling into the cauldron, should make the first head melt. But when the king's head fell into the cauldron nothing happened. Finally the stranger beheaded himself, and as his head fell into the cauldron all three fused together into a single lump. This was buried at the tumulus of the Three Kings. In some later versions of this story Mo Ye actually threw herself into the furnace in order that the metal should flow from the ore.

We are told that Gan Jiang hid the male sword in the mountains; this connection between mountains and swords is to be found elsewhere, also in a context that relates to the exercise of suzerainty (and, incidentally, of blood sacrifice). According to the *Zhe Ya*, certain swords of Yue were buried in order that they might acquire transcendental power. Once a year they were sprinkled with the blood of humans and of horses. At the time of rain their magical nature manifested itself in their attempts to escape from their sheaths, when they emitted a metallic sound. Zhao Tuo, king of Yue, buried swords of high repute in order to rule the famous mountains of his realm. That is why the mountains of Guangdong and Guangxi sometimes see the gleam of swords reflected in the midnight sky. Thus the sword is both a palladium and, it seems likely, an instrument in the king's apparatus for rain-making. This is not surprising, for there is considerable evidence in Chinese sources to suggest that, after the pattern of Yu, the smiths, makers of dynastic swords and challengers therefore of the imperial power, were also masters of the Thunder, controllers of the Seasons, and as ministers rivals before Heaven of the emperor himself. That to forge a pair of swords was to deal in matters of magical power is clearly shown in a story recorded in various Chinese sources, though it is attributed once more to Yue peoples.

There was once a barbarian chieftain called Fan Chui (his personal name means 'Hammer'), who had a slave called Fan Wen. One day when the latter was pasturing his master's sheep on the mountainside he found two carp in a stream. He hid them, intending to return later and eat the fish by himself. But his master learned of his find and ordered him to fetch the fish. Fan Wen, ashamed and frightened, claimed that he found two sharpening-stones, not fish at all. His master went to look, and when he came to the hiding place he found that there were indeed two sharpening-stones. Fan Wen then realised that there was something mysterious about the pair of carp. So he worked the stones, and from the metal he obtained from them forged two swords. Lifting the blades towards the Great Dyke (the mountains of the Annamite Chain), he cried: 'The carp are transformed into stones, the stones into swords by smelting. If there is power in them, let the rock be split, the dyke be broken. If I succeed I shall become ruler of this kingdom. If the swords do not enter the rock, then they are without power.' As he then advanced, the sword split the Great Dyke, and the people, seeing this, adhered to him. The sundered rock still exists, as do the swords, which have been handed down to his descendants from generation to generation.

Li hua long, 'the carp becomes a dragon', is a phrase used to describe success in the public examinations. The carp became a dragon by passing through the Dragon Gate, the pass in the mountains which was cleft by Yu the Great. And to assassinate a prince who is hard of access, the dagger should be concealed within a fish.

The Count of the River

All the rivers and streams of China had their deities and spirits, to whom offerings were made and about whom legends were recounted, but just as there was one river above all others, so there was one river-deity, He Bo, the Count of the River. Also known as Bingyi, he was the deity who controlled the Yellow River and the object of an official cult with sacrifices and offerings being made by the ruler. The Count was believed to have dedicated himself to the river by throwing himself in with a load of stones on his back: this act gave him magical power and gained him immortality.

The control of Hezong, the Ancestral Village of the River, became an object of dynastic struggles: the river was the life of China. The rulers of Qin called on the Count to witness their oaths, and when they gained control of Linzin they presented girls of royal blood to be his bride. All those who crossed the great river made offerings, but it was those who lived on its banks and made their living upon its waters who organised the great annual offerings. These were particularly centred at Linzin and Ye.

Until the ending of the Zhou dynasty the offerings included human sacrifices, each year seeing a girl offered to the Count as his bride. There was a college of sorcerers and sorceresses who managed the cult and the

Opposite. The Assembly of the Immortals by the Lake of Gems, or Green Jade Lake in the palace grounds of Xi Wang Mu. While some approach, others are seated on an island feasting on the peaches of immortality. Anonymous painting, late Ming. British Museum, London.

Below. Bronze *ding* decorated with hanging swords and cicadas, a vessel used for the preparation of sacrificial food and resembling the so-called tripod or cauldron of Yu, a symbol of dynastic power. The story of Gan Jiang and Mo Ye illustrates the themes of sacrifice connected with cauldrons, swords and royal power. Shang or Early Zhou. Minneapolis Institute of Arts, Minnesota. Bequest of Alfred B. Pillsbury.

offerings and who chose the bride. The chosen girl was proclaimed a year in advance; then, when the season was right, she was taken in bridal finery to a pavilion on the river bank. After feasting and a ritual fast she was placed upon a marriage bed and this was launched into the flooding stream, where the Count claimed his bride.

The sacrifices at Ye were ended by Simen Bao, an emissary of the Marquis Wen of Wei (427-387 B.C.), but those at Linzin continued until the time of Shi Huang Di. At Ye the emissary told the chief sorceress that the girl was not sufficiently beautiful to be the Count's bride. He then instructed his soldiers to throw the chief sorceress into the river to explain to the Count why the bride was delayed. When she did not return, he had a second and then a third sorceress thrown in on the same mission. Then, reflecting that women would not know how to explain, he had the regional head thrown in too. After this all those still on the bank banged their foreheads upon the ground until the blood flowed and their faces became ashen. Then the emissary stopped the ceremony, which was never resumed.

The Count of the River is capable of wrath, but sacrifice to him is to obtain his support, not his forgiveness. The Chu general Zeyu possessed a fine bonnet decorated with jade, which the deity coveted. He appeared therefore to the general in a dream and offered him victory over the prince of Qin in return for the hat. The general failed to comply and was defeated at Chengbo on the banks of the Yellow River.

Sacrifices to He Bo and his fellow river deities were one way of pleasing the waters, but there were other methods which could be used to deal with the great river. Then as now, the construction of dykes and dams and the cutting of canals were the methods recognised as most efficacious for flood-control and irrigation alike. And these skills were taught by Nugua, Gun and Yu, three of the most important characters to feature in Chinese mythology.

These myths we shall consider in

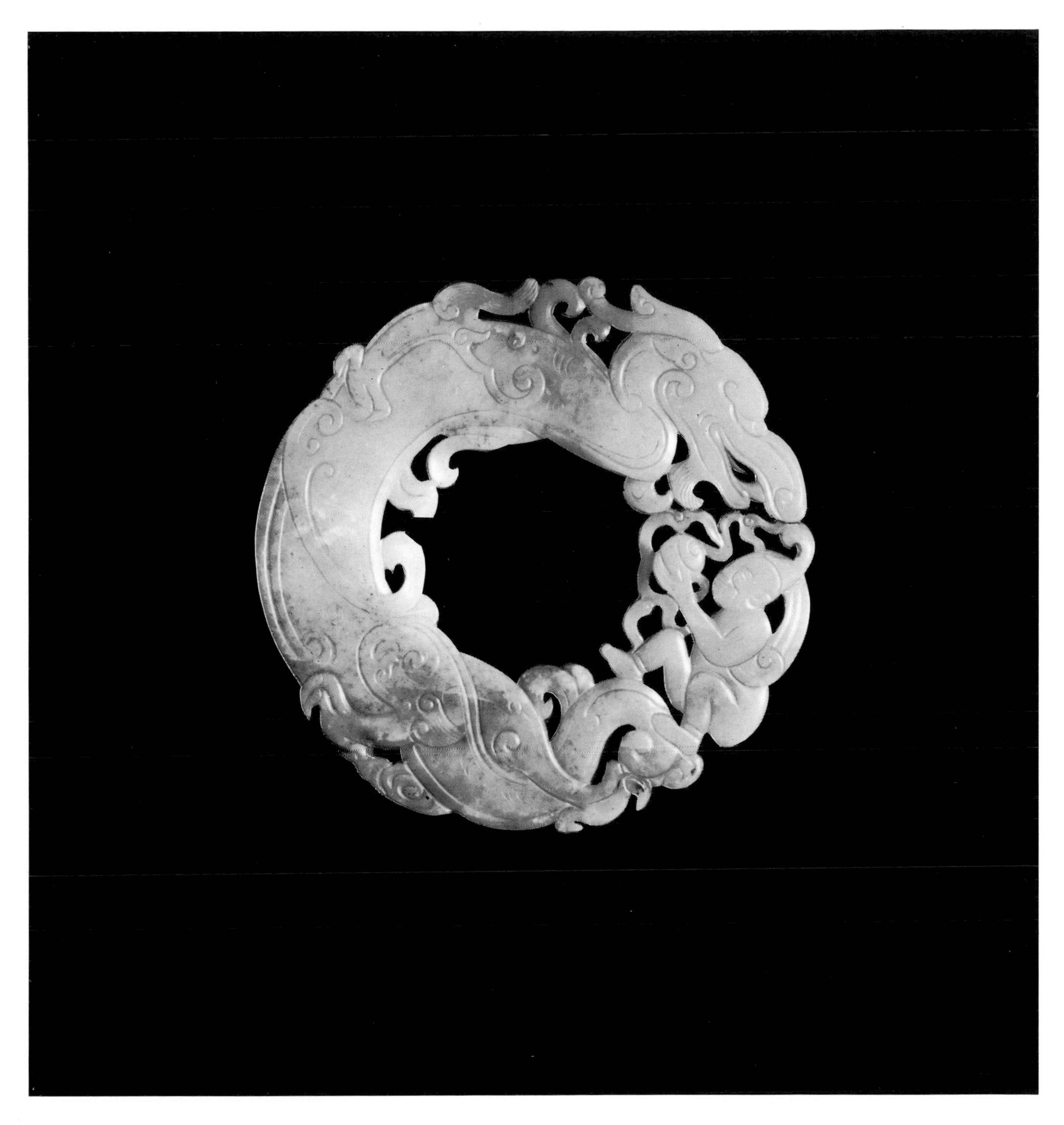

the next chapter, for they are part of the manner of life of the Chinese, for whom the flooding of their vast rivers is still a major problem. Here we may simply note that there is no question of the Flood in Chinese mythology being a universal punishment for human sin or wrong-doing. The rivers which overflow their banks are the result of some natural disaster that carries no implication of divine displeasure.

Above. Jade ring in the form of a dragon with a pearl held before its jaws. Highborn travellers cast such rings into the Yellow River as a placatory offering to He Bo, Count of the River, before venturing to make the crossing. Though originally human sacrifices were made, He Bo was said to be especially pleased with offerings of jade. British Museum, London.

Opposite. The Protector against Hail and Master of Thunder, who was especially worshipped by cultivators. As can be seen from his hammer and chisel he was a smith and thus, after the pattern of Yu, a controller of weather and of imperial power in rivalry with the Son of Heaven. Victoria and Albert Museum, London.

Following page. The spring fishing festival of south China villages, derived from the seasonal marriage festivals of prehistoric times and akin to the annual offerings made by fishing communities to He Bo, Count of the River. The dragon represents the ruler of the watery deep. Dish, *famille verte*, reign of Qian Long. Victoria and Albert Museum, London.

The Useful Arts

In the most ancient past, when people were few and animals many, human beings could not defend themselves against birds, beasts, insects or reptiles. A sage appeared at that time who made wooden nests to protect humans. The delighted people made him ruler of the world, calling him the Nest Builder. They lived on fruits, berries, mussels and clams, stinking and evil-smelling things which hurt their intestines so that they fell ill in large numbers. Then another sage appeared who used a fire-drill to produce fire which transformed the putrid, stinking food. The people made him ruler of the world under the name of Drill Man.

In the less remote past there was a great flood in the world, but Gun and Yu of the Xia dynasty opened up channels to control the water... When Yao ruled the world, his roof thatch was untrimmed and men did not plant speckled beans. He ate coarse millet and bitter green soup; his winter dress was deerskin, while for summer he wore rough fibres. Even a lowly gatekeeper was no

The tomb of the Tang princess Yong Tai, who was put to death by the Empress Zetian in A.D. 701 and reburied by her father after the empress's death, consists of a long passage leading to a stone burial chamber with stone sarcophagi, deep underground and covered with a high mound. The passage had niches in its walls which housed pottery figures of servants, over 700 in all. Fine metalwork and pottery were among the tomb furniture and the antechamber walls had paintings of young women dressed in the Persian manner with low-cut necks and narrow sleeves. The maids carry back-scratchers, sweetmeat boxes and fans. It was in the Tang period that exotica from abroad became the great delight of the court and its immediate circle. A.D. 706, near Xian.

Left. Rubbing from a stone relief in the tomb of the Wu family in Shandong, showing two calendar plants, the invention of Fuxi. The tree on the right grew one leaf every day for fifteen days, after which it lost one leaf a day; it thus measured the days of the month. The other tree grew a leaf every month for six months and then lost them one by one, thus marking the months of the year. Han dynasty. British Museum, London.

Opposite left. Nugua (left), holding compasses, and Fuxi, holding a set-square. By inventing marriage and a *yin-yang* partnership with Fuxi, Nugua re-established cosmic equilibrium after Gong-gong's destructive attack. Below is Dong Wang Gong with two winged servants who are preparing a drug of immortality. The three-fold support is based on the character *shan*, mountain. Pillar of a tomb at Bei Zhai Cun.

Opposite right. Jurong, Spirit of Fire and heavenly executioner, who was alternatively the third son of the deity of Tai Shan, or the son of one of the mythical emperors, who instructed him to keep order on earth. He killed both Gong-gong, for bringing floods, and Kun, for stealing the means to control them. He was especially honoured by the emperors of the tenth and eleventh centuries. Victoria and Albert Museum, London.

worse clothed and provided for than he. When Yu ruled the world, he led his people with plough and spade, working until there was no further down on his thighs or hair upon his shins. . . In the time of Shun, the Miao tribes were unsubmissive and Yu proposed to attack them. Shun said: 'It will not do, for to take up arms while the ruler's virtue is unperfected would be a violation of the Way.' Then Shun taught good government for three years. After this he took up shield and battleaxe and performed the war dance, whereupon Miao submitted. But in the war with the Gong-gong tribe men used iron lances with steel points that reached as far as the enemy, so that a man without stout helmet and armour was likely to be wounded.

Such is the account which Han Fei Zi gives of the early stages of Chinese cultural history. Other accounts tell of the inventions and discoveries assigned to the various rulers and sovereigns in pre-Xia times, or to their ministers. The most extensive set of stories is that which deals with the control of floods and the development of irrigation which, in legend, began with the moment when Gong-gong, defeated in his attempt to wrest sovereignty of the world from Yao, overturned Mount Buzhou, tilting the earth and causing the rivers to flood. But this is only one of a number of flood stories, so that we find many confusions in the surviving textual versions of the myths and legends. It is to some of these we will now turn our attention.

Nugua and Fuxi

We have already met the goddess Nugua as a creator of mankind. But her services as a restorer of order to the world after the attack on Mount Bu Zou are equally important in the cycle of stories about her, even though it does not seem that the original version of the legend was about Gong-gong at all. It may well have concerned a quite other monster who became assimilated to him when scholars tried to produce some version to reconcile traditions of different ethnic and cultural groups during China's formative period.

In early sources Nugua occurs alone, but later she is always associated with Fuxi, who, in the traditional account of pre-dynastic China, is the first of the Three Sovereigns preceding the Five Emperors. She is either his younger sister, or, once she has invented marriage, his wife. The conflict between her role as sister and wife is, however, by no means absolute, for in the myths of non-Chinese tribes in the south we find that it is from the incestuous intercourse of brother and sister that a new race of men is created after a destructive flood has eliminated mankind. As a pair, Fuxi and Nugua are first represented in Han times as beings with human bodies and dragon tails, which are intertwined to link them. He carries a set-square, she compasses: the latter are round, representing sky, while the former is square, representing earth. Once again we are in the presence of the male-female, *yin-yang* system. Together compasses (*gui*) and set-square (*ju*) symbolise *guiju*: order, proper conduct. To restore the devastation caused by Gong-gong's violence is

to re-establish pattern in the world.

In the *Liezi* the account of Nugua's achievement reads thus:

'In oldest times the four cardinal points were out of place; the Nine Provinces lay open; the sky did not wholly cover the earth; the earth did not wholly support the sky; fire burnt ceaselessly without dying out; the waters flowed on without ceasing; wild beasts devoured the peaceful people, birds of prey carried off the aged and children. Then Nugua smelted the stones of five colours to make good the azure sky; she cut off the feet of a tortoise to fix the cardinal points; she slew the black dragon to save the country of Chi; she piled up ashes of reeds to stop the overflowing waters. All was tranquil at that time: everything was at peace.'

This summary account of the activities of the goddess is full of difficulties, but one thing is clear: her task is to restore order. In another text the waters are described as licentious and needing to be brought back into a system of equilibrium. The reference to fire which burns ceaselessly while the waters overflow may relate to another part of the story of Gong-gong, where the Spirit of Fire, Jurong, was sent to punish the monster but failed in his task. (As we shall see later, however, the Fire Spirit was called in to punish another hero figure who tried to stop flooding.) The islands of the Eastern Sea rested upon tortoises, though these had feet. It may be that the concept of stability, embodied in the tortoise, which here requires cardinal pillars, can only be expressed by the use of a tortoise part, the leg, for the whole. The commentators say that the ash of reeds is efficacious in the repair of breached dykes because

reeds grow in water. It may be that the concept of reed (water) and ash (fire) is also seen as an expression of harmonious union or *yin-yang*. Such an idea is certainly hidden in the reference to the stones of five colours, for these appear in a number of texts, often relating to the forging of magic swords or cauldrons whose power depends upon the combination of the five ores in a proper and harmonious alloy. The black dragon which here threatens Chi, an allusion that seems to belong to another story, is a rain demon, whose fault is presumably excess of zeal. Some commentators have claimed that the black dragon is Gong-gong, but there is no reason to agree.

Yao and Gun

There is another flood legend which is considerably more circumstantial and which contains the history of the origins of hydraulic engineering. This is set in the time of the emperor Yao, when the overflowing waters reached up to the sky. Yao sought the advice of Four-Mountains, who bade him ask the help of Gun, the great grandson of Huang Di, who is sometimes described as having the form of a white horse. Yao was reluctant to do so, but in the end agreed. Gun set about his task by building dams, but these collapsed under the weight of the waters before they were strong enough to confine them. A tortoise, some say it was three-footed, and a horned owl appeared, and advised Gun to steal the Swelling Earth from Huang Di. This alone could block the waters and confine them in seemly manner. Gun took their counsel and stole the magic earth, which had the property of growing ceaselessly. With its aid he began to control the waters and thus incurred the wrath of Huang Di. The latter sent Jurong, Spirit of Fire and heavenly executioner, to dispose of Gun, as he had once been sent to punish Gong-gong for causing a flood. Jurong slew Gun on Feather Mountain. This punishment took place in the sixty-ninth year of Yao's reign, after Gun had toiled for nine years. Some say that Gun was torn to pieces by tortoises and owls, but in fact his body lay as it was in life and did not decompose. Finally after three years, his belly was slashed open with the sword of Wu and there

Right. Supernatural being, possibly Four-Mountains, guardian of the four quarters of the universe, and counsellor of Yao, one of the Five Emperors. His presence at court symbolised the emperor's possession of his realm. Earthenware figure from a tomb, Tang dynasty. Victoria and Albert Museum, London.

Opposite. In early China burials of rulers and nobles were accompanied by human and animal sacrifices, no doubt to provide service for the dead in the afterlife. Such victims were slowly replaced by models, some in the tomb and others to line the ceremonial ways which led to the grave. In Ming times such figures were often of gigantic size. A similar practice developed in Vietnam where Ming practices were adopted by the rulers.

emerged his son Yu in the form of a winged and horned dragon. Gun turned into a yellow bear and threw himself into the river, though there are accounts which say he became a three-footed tortoise or a yellow dragon.

Yu, Master of Floods

Yu, learning from his father's misfortune, went to see Huang Di in Heaven and obtained from him permission to use the Swelling Earth. He was thus equipped to accept the invitation of Shun, who had succeeded Yao some two years earlier, to control the floods. In some accounts Huang Di gave to Yu as much Swelling Earth as could be piled on to the back of a black tortoise and also ordered the Winged Dragon to assist him. Yu began his task by damming the springs from which the waters came: there were 233,559 of these, but with the Swelling Earth he could block them all. Then he built mountains at the corners of the earth to ensure that there would be regions that could not be submerged. They also served to anchor what was otherwise in danger of being swept away by the floods. Of course, there were inevitably small openings which escaped even Yu's thorough labours and it is because of these that there are still floods. The mountains nevertheless ensure that the floods are never so engulfing as in the time before Yu began his task. There still remained the problem of the water already on the earth. With the tail of the Winged Dragon Yu now cut ditches by which the water was guided back into the river beds, whence it flowed to the sea; but sometimes mere ditches were not enough and Yu had to tunnel through mountains or split them in order to make a passage for the great waters on their journey to the sea.

After Yu had toiled for many years he reached the age of thirty when, according to Confucian tradition, it was proper to take a wife. One day, as he thought of this, he approached a clump of willows from which he saw a white fox with nine tails appear. This reminded him of a prophecy that to see such a beast was to guarantee sovereignty, while to marry the girl of Du Shan was to obtain a flourishing lineage. He made his way to Mount Du, where he found a girl waiting for him: her name was also Dushan. They were married and she accompanied Yu in his work. One day he was engaged in tunnelling through a mountain, a task which he carried out by transforming himself into a bear. Now it was his custom, when he was ready for his food, to summon Dushan by beating upon a drum: on this day he fell against a stone which sounded like the drum. His wife hurried to him and saw a great bear from whom she fled in terror. As she ran in panic Yu pursued her, still in the form of a bear. Slowly he overtook her, but as he was on the point of reaching her, she turned into a rock. Now Yu knew that she was pregnant and as she underwent this transformation, he

begged her to leave him their child. The rock split on the north side and a boy was born called Qi ('Split').

It was Qi, who in succeeding his father as ruler of Xia, established for the first time in China the rule of primogeniture. According to Sima Qian, Yu had nominated his minister Bo-yi as his successor but the feudal lords deserted him and came to support Qi, saying that their prince was the son of the sovereign Yu. In another tradition Qi is said to have slain Bo-yi and seized power: there may be in this some recollection of an older system whereby a minister exercised power during the period of mourning between one ruler and the next, a three-year interregnum after which the minister was supposed to instal a legitimate successor to exercise full suzerainty. Qi rode upon two dragons, who were able to transport him on visits to Heaven. There he heard divine music and it was by this means that men learnt to compose music.

Although he had lost his wife in this dramatic fashion, Yu's work was not yet complete. There were still monsters to be slain and works to be accomplished. He fought against a vassal of Gong-gong called Xiangyao, a serpent-bodied creature with nine heads, whose pastureland was nine mountains and whose vomit formed evil springs and marshes. When Yu slew him, his foul blood corrupted the fields and the crops would not grow. Where his body lay there was so great a flood that the land was uninhabitable. Yu tried to clear up the mess by containing it within a dyke (as his predecessor had tried unsuccessfully to control Gong-gong's flood by embankments). Thrice he built the walls and thrice they were breached. Then he dug a lake and was successful. In the middle of this lake Yu built a tower, some say with the earth from the excavations for the lake. This set a pattern for later times when the erection of a tower was held to be efficacious for the control of dragons.

It is probably in his capacity of master of floods that Yu is said to have received from the Count of the River a river map which, it is sometimes said, was placed on the back of a horse. The gift is sometimes made to Fuxi, the inventor of trigrams – which were, in fact, the symbols employed on the map. Yu and Fuxi are linked in various ways, for according to another story, Yu, while engaged in his channelling of the waters, penetrated a deep cavern in whose interior he discovered Fuxi with his human face and serpent body. The latter presented Yu with a jade slab fashioned into a scale for measuring Heaven and Earth. This refers to another of Yu's functions, for he traversed all the earth and its waters, measuring them and determining the directions and distances. Thus in one version it seems to be implied that he was responsible for the construction of the cardinal mountains. In the chapter of the *Shu jing* known as the Tribute of Yu there are accounts of Yu's supposed activities in delineating the empire and its peoples and products. In these descriptions the real and the mythical are apparently given the same credence. The text presumably dates from the fifth century B.C., but represents a much older tradition. It is interesting to note that since Yu has to travel to carry out the task of describing the land he is also credited with the invention of various means of transport. In this system the earth is square: the distance between each of the cardinal poles 233,575 paces, the figures having been established either by Yu himself or by his two assistants, Dazhang and Shouhai.

The knowledge of the earth's geography was translated by Yu into a tangible record which became the palladium of the Xia, the so-called Nine Cauldrons. Traditionally these were cast by Yu himself from metal

Left above. A winged dragon. This was the form in which Yu was born. The winged dragon aided Huang Di in his struggle against the rebel Chiyu, son of Shennong, and on Huang Di's instructions became the instrument with which Yu cut ditches to channel the floodwaters. Probably the handle of a vessel. Sixth to fifth century B.C. British Museum, London.

Left. The serpent-bodied sovereign Fuxi, who taught people how to fish, to domesticate animals, and to breed silkworms, and to whom the first dragon appeared in 2962 B.C. He invented trigrams, the basis of writing and scholarship, as well as music and the instrument with which Yu measured, and so encompassed, the universe. Painting on silk of the Qian Long period (1736-95). Metropolitan Museum of Art, New York. Gift of Mrs Edward S. Harkness, 1947.

Opposite. Yu, master of floods, who by working continuously for thirteen years at this great task of flood control earned a high reputation for selfless devotion to duty, and became emperor in succession to Shun. Yu founded the Xia dynasty despite his own wishes: the people ignored his nomination of his minister to succeed him and installed his son Qi on the throne. Yu was thus the first king to be succeeded by his son. Painting by Ma Lin. Song dynasty. National Palace Museum, Taipei.

brought from far-off countries by the Nine Shepherds. It appears that each cauldron bore representations of provincial symbols and thus subsumed all the beings, and products, of the region in question, together with some kind of map. The cauldrons were cast when the Xia dynasty was at its most powerful. As the dynasty declined, so the weight of the cauldrons decreased. They could thus be more easily borne off or even transport themselves, a capacity which they owed to the Female Tortoise of the North, whose head faced to the right and who had been consulted on the occasion of their being cast. The whole of the tradition regarding the cauldrons seems to link Yu with clans of miners, the possible connection being through the mountains: here Yu had dug passes for the easier dispersal of the waters, just as the miners dug their galleries for ores. Each dynasty possessed cauldrons of this type and similar vessels were to be found in the contiguous regions under Chinese influence. Those of the Nguyen dynasty survived until recently at their capital Hue in Vietnam.

In his capacity as caster of the Nine Cauldrons, Yu the Great was a smith. Granet has shown, in masterly fashion, how important in the cultural

Left. The ox-headed divine farmer Shennong, second of the Three Sovereigns, who taught humans the arts of agriculture as well as the use of herbal drugs. He was also god of the burning wind, and during his reign the people were saved from drought only by the intervention of Chi Songzi, who became the Lord of Rain, and who later sided with Shennong's son against Huang Di. Engraving from *Sanzai tuhui* (1607 edition). University of Hong Kong.

Opposite. A guardian figure from a Tang tomb. Figures of this type seem to have developed from pottery images of a Han genie, *fangxiang,* which were placed in tombs, sometimes in each corner. The original genie repelled sickness and evil: whether their function in the tomb was to protect the living or the dead is unknown. In post-Han times they seem to have become assimilated to the Four Kings of Heaven of popular Buddhism, whose role was also largely protective. Victoria and Albert Museum, London.

history of China were confraternities of craftsmen, mainly smiths, which seem to have grown out of groups of husbandmen who developed specialist skills. And it was in such fraternities that agricultural techniques appear to have developed.

Shennong

The successor to Nugua, the ox-headed Shennong, is said to have invented the plough and to have taught men basic agriculture, but it seems likely that he was first and foremost god of the burning wind, of the technique of clearing scrub jungle by fire in order to set seeds in the area, rich in potash, which remains after the fire has passed. If this is so, then one can understand that, as planting replaces gathering and ploughing replaces slash-and-burn, the new inventions called for by new techniques are attributed to the originally presiding deity.

Huang Di and Chiyu

Shennong's son, minister or grandson – the texts are wonderfully confused – was called Chiyu. Like Shennong, he was ox-headed, with sharp horns, a bronze forehead and iron skull. His temples were covered with hair which bristled like swords. He was the inventor of war and of weapons, and fought against Huang Di (either the Yellow Emperor or the August Sovereign: the text are ambiguous and reflect the confusion of innumerable conflations). The struggle between Huang Di and Chiyu is a classic example of the struggle between ruler and rebel (who is often a minister in revolt). Both sides had the aid of celestial creatures: the Winged Dragon sided with Huang Di, the Count of the Wind and the Master of Rain with Chiyu. When Chiyu called down thick fog to confuse the fighting, Huang Di invented the compass so as to guide his own forces. The horns upon which his troops blew made the sound of dragons. Ultimately Huang Di summoned from Heaven the goddess Ba, who, in the eyes of some, was his daughter, and bade her drive off the rain and wind. Being drought, she was able to do so. Chiyu was defeated and beheaded, but Ba, the goddess of drought, stayed upon earth for reasons which are not clear, and that is why drought still inflicts itself upon mankind. Despite her previous assistance to him, Huang Di was forced in the end to send her into exile so that humanity might survive.

This series of tales illustrates an important conceptual pattern for the transfer of power from one dynasty to the next: Chiyu is the son of Shennong and a minister; Huang Di must overcome him in order that he may succeed to the throne as the first of the Five Emperors. Both are leaders of confraternities represented by their acolytes: Drought and Rain Dragon, Wind and Rain. But in the time before Huang Di the basic elements of Chinese existence had been expounded to the human race: the floods controlled, the earth measured and mapped, and the plough and agriculture made available.

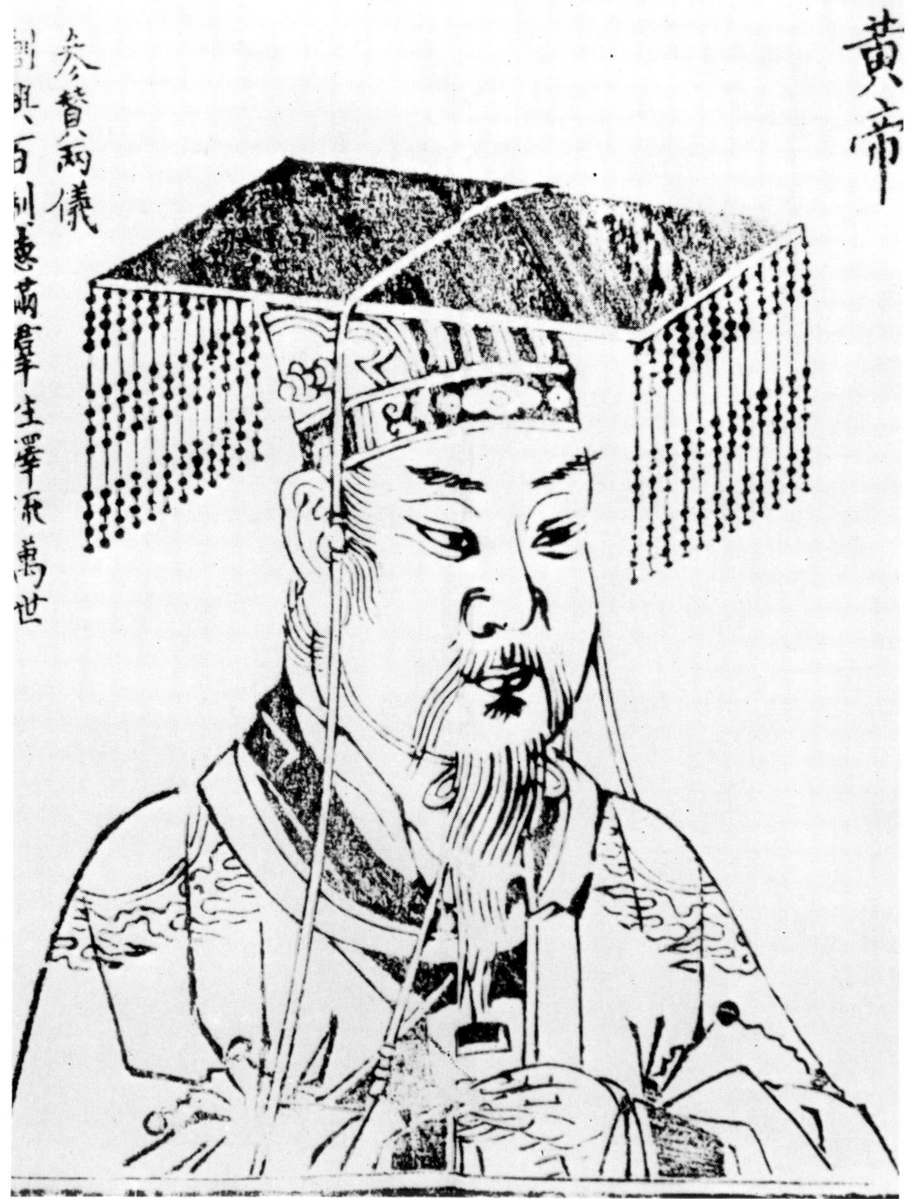

Huang Di, the Yellow Emperor, first of the Five Emperors who was credited with the invention of the chariot wheel and potter's wheel as well as the compass. When his rebel minister Chiyu invented war and weapons, Huang Di resisted him with these inventions and with ships and armour, which he introduced to the human race. From *Lidai guren xiangzan* (1498 edition). University of Hong Kong.

Peasant Myths

Side by side with these formal myths, reflecting no doubt scholarly politickings in support of factional interests, we find popular tales which give accounts of specific discoveries in the realm of agriculture and the like. Such stories represent a tradition that the scholars either overlooked or thought unworthy of their attention.

The Ox, Helper of Farmers

In general, the popular tales are not concerned with cosmogonies or with attempts to construct cosmologies. If they deal with origins, it is with the origin of useful things, as we shall observe. Sometimes they are tinged with elements from one or other of the faiths which have from time to time spread through China. A good example of this is to be seen in the versions of the story of how humans were provided with plough-oxen.

In the past people had to struggle for food. Despite the fact that they worked day and night, it was only on every third or fourth day, sometimes even less frequently, that they were able to eat. This state of affairs distressed the Emperor of Heaven, who sent down the Ox star from the sky to tell human beings that if they were to work hard and diligently, then they would always be able to eat every third day. But the Ox was stupid: he went hastily down to earth and told people that the Emperor of Heaven had decreed that they should eat three times a day. Since the Ox had made a mistake in his instructions, he was sent back to earth to help with the ploughing, for with only their own hands and feet it would not have been possible for men to prepare sufficient food. That is why plough-oxen, originally found only in heaven, exist on earth.

In a Buddhist version of the story Dizang, Ksitigarbha Bodhisattva, who is believed to rule over Hell, was

The Five Buddhas. Though formally subordinate to the native religions, Buddhism captured the imagination and was assimilated to some of the oldest beliefs. The Five Buddhas correspond to the Great Emperors of the Five Peaks and are associated with the Daoist symbolism of the five elements. Buddhist scroll painting, late seventeenth century A.D. Religionskundliche Sammlung der Universität, Marburg.

aroused to compassion by the struggle for food. This story also explains why the Bodhisattva is ruler of Hell and indicates how Buddhist deities are subordinate to 'native' China ones. The Bodhisattva suggested to the Jade Emperor that the heavenly Ox should be sent down to earth to aid humanity in the preparation of the fields. But the Jade Emperor would not agree for he knew that while people would care for the ox so long as it was able to pull the plough, once it was too feeble they would kill it, eat its flesh and tan its hide. This the Bodhisattva disputed. He pledged that if such a thing were to happen he would suffer banishment to Hell. Of course things turned out as the Jade Emperor had feared: as soon as the ox was too feeble to pull the plough, its flesh was eaten, its hide stripped off and used. And though the ox pleaded with its ungrateful users, they remained unmoved. Then the Jade Emperor was angry and banished Dizang Busa to Hell, where as an additional punishment he had to keep his eyes closed except on the thirtieth day of the seventh month. And so it is that on that day people light candles and burn incense in his honour.

The Origins of Crops

We have already seen that agriculture and its techniques were the invention of the pre-Yin rulers of China, at least in so far as the formal myths are concerned. There are many different stories, however, about the origins of specific plants and the like.

The Introduction of Rice

According to one of these the rice plant existed from the beginning but its ears were not filled. This was the time when people lived by hunting and gathering. The goddess Guan Yin saw that people lived in hardship and near starvation. She was moved to pity and resolved to help them. She went secretly into the ricefields and squeezed her breasts so that the milk flowed into the ears of the rice plants. Almost all of them were filled, but to complete her task she had to press so hard that a mixture of milk and blood flowed into the plants. That is why there are two kinds of rice, the white from the milk, the red from the mixture of milk and blood.

In another story rice is the gift of a dog. After the floods had been controlled by Yu, people found that all the old plants had been destroyed, but that no new ones had taken their place. So they had to live by hunting. One day a dog was seen to emerge from a waterlogged field. From its tail there hung bunches of long yellow ears full of seeds, which people planted in the wet, but drained fields. The seeds grew and the plants ripened to give the people rice. For this they were very grateful to the dog, so before eating they always offered a little food to the dog and at the first meal after the rice-harvest the food was shared with the dog.

Right. Guan Yin seated on Budo Shan, the famous Buddhist sanctuary in the Jusan islands to which the goddess was borne on a water lily. Despite her expression of abstraction, Guan Yin was loved beyond the other deities, for she postponed her own eternal bliss to help human beings and had mercy on all who called upon her. Buddhist scroll painting, *c.* eighteenth to nineteenth century A.D. Religionskundliche Sammlung der Universität, Marburg.

Opposite. Ploughing a ricefield with an ox. The human race learnt the art of ploughing from the ox-headed mythical emperor Shennong, but the grains of rice were not filled until Guan Yin took pity on the starving, and humans would have been unable to produce enough food if the plough-ox had not come down from heaven to help. Jade screen, reign of Kang Xi (1662-1722). Seattle Art Museum, Washington.

The Lobu Radish

Sometimes stories of this kind are also edifying moralities, such as one from central China which tells of the origin of the red-cored radish, *lobu*. This relates how Mulien, a good and virtuous man, suffered on account of his mother, a lazy scold who killed many animals to eat. When Mulien reproached his mother for taking life, she cursed him, an act which caused him much grief. One day Mulien's mother fell ill and knew that she was going to die. She told her son that, as a punishment for having put to death so many living things, she knew that her soul would be banished to Hell for ever. On her death her dutiful son spent all his fortune on priests to recite prayers to save his mother from Hell. When the money was finished, he became a monk and devoted himself to the same cause. By his merit and virtue he became a Buddha and was then able to descend into Hell to rescue his mother. He seized her in his arms and ran with her until, exhausted by his efforts, he was forced to lie down by the side of a field. His mother, whose punishment in Hell had included starvation, saw that there were radishes in the field and, pulling one up, ate it. Mulien was appalled, for if the deity of Heaven noticed the theft it would lead to his mother's return to Hell for all eternity. So he cut off his finger and pushed it into the hole left by the stolen vegetable, where it grew as a red-cored radish. Mulien, who thus exemplified the virtue of filial piety, was the Buddhist teacher Maudgalyayana, whose personal name in folk mythology is Lo Bu, which probably explains why he is credited with the origin of the *lobu* radish.

The Creation of Opium

An interesting story occurs in various forms to account for the origins of

opium, tobacco or betel. The story tells of a man with a very ugly wife who upset him so that he could do nothing but curse her and threaten to throw her out. The wife accepted his ill-treatment, for she loved him dearly; but finally she fell ill of despair. As the hour of her death approached she said to her husband that despite the evil way in which he had treated her, he would realise after her death how much she loved him. About a week after her burial the husband learnt that a beautiful white flower had appeared on her grave. Within the flower was a small round fruit. This curious phenomenon worried the widower, who remembered the dying woman's words and began to regret his ill-behaviour. He wondered whether she had turned into a plant in order to injure him. Finally thoughts of his dead wife so filled his mind that he could neither sleep nor work. He fell ill, but he had no children to care for him, nor could the doctors help him. Then one night his wife appeared to him in a dream. She told him that the plant on her grave was formed from her soul: from a cut in the central fruit a juice would appear which, once it had hardened, could be smoked in a pipe. If her husband smoked the juice every day he would be relieved of his suffering. In the morning he did just this and with the first pipeful his suffering was eased. Thus the wife redeemed her dying pledge to prove her love.

The Discovery of Salt

Another story deals with the discovery of salt, a commodity not only valued for itself but also of great importance in the imperial revenue system. One day a poor peasant working in fields by the seashore saw a phoenix perched on a mound on the edge of the sea. As he knew that there was always treasure buried where a phoenix perched, as soon as the bird flew away he began to dig on the spot. He found nothing but some curious earth and concluded that it must be of value. He took it home with him hoping to make his fortune with it; but then he reflected that to fail to report finding treasure to the emperor was to incur the death penalty. Obviously he could not risk marketing his find. He decided therefore to report his discovery at court. He duly presented himself before the emperor and told of the circumstances which led to his appearing with the rather unpleasantly smelling clod of earth. The emperor was not pleased and, accusing the wretched man of wasting his time, ordered his immediate execution.

The piece of earth was forgotten on a shelf. But it was the wet season and one day as the cook was passing by with a dish for the emperor's meal a drop from the moist clod fell into the food. There was no time to prepare another dish, so the cook placed the contaminated one before his master. The latter at the first taste recognised that the food was incomparably finer than any he had tasted before and demanded an explanation from the cook. He, not daring to dissemble, had to admit that there had been an accident between kitchen and table. The emperor, wondering whether after all the peasant's discovery was of value, sampled the juice that ran from the clod of earth on his food. There was no doubt: the flavours were immeasurably enhanced. Then orders were given for the mound to be exploited and it was found that the earth could be moistened and then dried to produce flavour-enhancing crystals. Nothing could be done for the peasant, but his son was appointed to a high post and grew rich.

The Pumpkin Girl and the Great Wall

Among the many folktales collected by Lin Lan, there can be little doubt that the best known is that of Meng Jiang Nu. Its widespread popularity is the result of its frequent use in theatrical pieces from the time of the Ming dynasty onwards, but the story is very much older. Indeed, as Gu Jiegang has shown, the original story goes back to pre-Han times: when the theme was made to centre about the construction of the Great Wall of China, completed by Qin Shi Huang Di in the third century B.C.. The form of the story was already well established, with its emphasis on loyalty and adherence to a husband in disgrace. In the form recorded by Lin Lan, the story combines a number of motifs from different sources and provides a good example of an evolved Chinese folkstory.

The land of the Meng family was separated from that of the Jiang by a wall. In one year the two families each planted a climbing pumpkin by the wall, and when the plants grew they met at the wall top and joined together. From this union an enormous fruit grew. When it had ripened it was gathered by the two families together, for after much discussion as to the ownership of the plant, it had been agreed that each family should have a half of the fruit. When it was divided, however, they found inside a beautiful little girl. They agreed to bring her up jointly and called her Meng Jiang, from the names of the two foster families.

This was in the time when Shi Huang Di of the Qin dynasty, fearful of Hunnish threats against the empire, had resolved to build a wall along the northern frontier of China. But as soon as a section of the wall was completed it collapsed. Finally a sage advised the emperor that it was necessary to immure a living human victim at each mile (1.5 kilometres) of the wall's 10-thousand mile (16,000-kilometre) length. The emperor adopted his advice and the empire lived in terror as the demand for victims grew. Then another scholar went to the emperor and suggested a method that would provide the necessary number of offerings without imposing further terror on the people. What was needed was to sacrifice a man called Wan, for since the name Wan meant 'ten thousand', his

The goddess Guan Yin, enthroned on a lotus rising from the waters. She was the Chinese form of the Bodhisattva Avalokitesvara, who by the Tang dynasty had become a female goddess of mercy and bringer of children, identified with an ancient Chinese mother-goddess. Her milk, compassionately given to the human race, filled the ears of the rice plant. Eighteenth-century scroll painting. Wellcome Institute for the Ministry of Medicine, London.

sacrifice would meet the requirements of the spirits which were destroying the wall as it was built. The delighted emperor sent at once for Wan, but the latter had heard of the proposal and had fled. Now it so happened that he was hiding in a tree in the garden of Meng Jiang's house when she went out by moonlight to bathe in the pool there. In her pleasure she said, 'If any man were to see me now, as I am naked, then I would happily belong to him for ever.' And Wan called out from his tree, 'I have seen you.' So Meng Jiang and he were married. In the course of their wedding feast, soldiers came and seized Wan, leaving his bride in tears and the marriage unconsummated.

Though Meng Jiang had never known her husband, she was as bound to him in memory as any other wife would have been, and she undertook a perilous journey to the Great Wall in search of her husband's bones. But when she reached the wall she was appalled at its length, and did not know where she should begin her search. As she sat and wept, the wall took pity on her and collapsed to reveal the remains of her husband.

Now when the emperor heard of Meng Jiang's devoted search, he wished to see her; and when he did so he was so struck by her beauty that he determined to make her his empress. When Meng Jiang learned of this inescapable decision she agreed, subject to three conditions: there should be a forty-nine day funerary feast in honour of her husband; the emperor and the high officials of the court should attend the ceremonies; and an altar 49 *chi* (17.5 metres) high should be erected by the riverbank where she might make offerings to her dead husband. Qin Shi Huang Di consented without demur.

When all had been made ready as Meng Jiang had required, she mounted upon the high altar in the presence of the emperor and his court, and began to revile him for all his cruelty and evil. But the emperor took no action. Then she threw herself from the altar into the river. At this the emperor could restrain himself no longer, but bade his soldiers drag her from the water, cut her body into pieces, and grind her bones to dust. And when they did so, the pieces turned into little silver-coloured fish in which the soul of the faithful Meng Jiang continues to live.

Cai the Brickmaker

The theme of human sacrifice in order to bring about the completion of a

Above. Rice seedlings being prepared for transplantation. They will be set out in well-spaced rows to grow to maturity in carefully regulated irrigated fields.

Opposite. Woven silk tapestry showing a pair of phoenixes in a landscape of rocks and peonies. The phoenix was believed, in popular mythology, to be associated with buried treasure. A pair of them are generally held to symbolise felicity. The work is an example of a technique called *kosi*, cut silk, probably invented in Central Asia and perfected in Song China, in which a needle is used as a shuttle to produce a weave substantially finer than that of the finest Gobelins. This example is A.D. fifteenth to sixteenth century. Victoria and Albert Museum, London.

piece of work is by no means uncommon in Chinese myths and legends. Eberhard records an interesting story from Zhejiang in which such an event is related about brickmaking. It is uncertain how late into historical times such sacrifices actually took place, but we have already noted the frequent occurrence of human sacrifices in Shang times, both in funerary contexts and in connection with important buildings. The Zhejiang story seems to belong to a stage at which the shift from human to animal sacrifices had already taken place.

There was once a village of brick-makers. The villages were generally prosperous and careful to maintain good relations with the god of the brick-kilns. Whenever a new kiln was brought into use, a pig and a sheep were sacrificed in front of the furnace door in honour of the deity. To omit the offering was to risk the production of soft, yellow bricks which could not find a market, or even the collapse of the whole kiln. Now though the villagers lived on good terms with one another, there was one man, Cai, who was determined to acquire control of the whole business of the village. To do this he built a vast new kiln a little distance away, but when it came to be fired the out-turn of bricks was quite useless: all were soft and yellow. Neither the builders of the kiln nor his own workmen could suggest any reason for this, but finally one old man suggested that a fortune-teller should be consulted. This was agreed and an answer obtained. It appeared that the traditional sacrifices were insufficient in Cai's case, because of his evil heart. The god of the kiln would be satisfied with nothing less than the sacrifice of the would-be monopolist's daughter.

Cai went at once to a far off village and there bought a thirteen-year-old girl as a substitute for his own daughter, a girl of the same age who was at the time living with the family into which she was in due course to marry. Cai brought back his true daughter and the girl he had purchased – they were strikingly alike – and lodged them together until the time of the sacrifical feast. In order that the bought girl should not learn of her true destiny, Cai ordered her to eat and to sleep with his daughter on the eve of the sacrifice. Few knew of Cai's intentions, but he instructed some of his workmen that when the girl arrived in the morning with their breakfast they should cast her alive into the furnace of the kiln and, afterwards, sacrifice the usual sheep and pig in front of the furnace door. Then he told the girl to go to bed early and to rise early the next morning in order to bring food to the workmen and to summon them to the sacrifice.

The two girls went to bed, but it was Cai's daughter, over-excited at the thought of the sacrifical feast, who could not sleep. And it was she who slipped out early the next morning to bring the workmen their breakfast and summon them to the sacrifice. The workmen, forewarned by Cai, were awaiting the girl, so as soon as his daughter arrived they cast her alive into the furance. In the meantime Cai had gone to the girls' room to waken the one he had purchased and to send her on her way to her death before anyone else stirred. He was appalled to find no sign of his daughter and hastened to the kiln in time to be met by the workmen on their way to report that orders had been carried out. The wretched man, overcome by grief, broke down and wept.

Popular Myths of the Great Gods

There are, naturally, many popular tales about deities, not all of them particularly respectful. Some certainly derive from Buddhist canonical sources, or later tales devised as glosses upon the canon. Others seem to be simple expressions of the peasant's eternal hope for better things in a future existence. A typical version of such a story is to be found in a tale from central China quoted by Eberhard, which explains how the kitchen-god came to be appointed.

The Kitchen-God

The kitchen-god was once no more than a poor mason who seemed fated to be unsuccessful all his life. At last his circumstances became so utterly

desperate that he was forced to sell his wife into marriage with another man. Now it so happened that one day he went to work for the man who had become his wife's new husband, but he no longer recognised her. His wife, however, still had him much in mind and, although she could not help him overtly, she resolved to do so by stealth. She baked some sesame cakes and into each one she placed a piece of money, for her new family was quite well-to-do. When he came to leave, having finished the work for which he had been called, she gave him the cakes for his journey home, but did not mention their secret ingredient. On the way the mason stopped at a wayside teahouse to break his journey. Here another traveller asked him for one of the cakes, a request which the mason gladly agreed to. The other bit into the cake and found the money, but said nothing to the mason about it. Instead, he persuaded him to part with the rest of the cakes for a modest sum. The mason, in accordance with his characteristic ill-fortune, thus parted with the gift that his ex-wife had given him out of love, while thinking that he had done well to have obtained a modest amount for the cakes. Later, when he learnt what his wife had done, he recognised that there was no point in his continued existence. He therefore killed himself. But the ruler of Heaven, acknowledging his honesty and goodness, appointed him as the kitchen-deity.

The Two Gods of the Soil

Another tale shows deities in a somewhat odd light. It appears that there were once two gods of the soil, one on the northern mountain in a certain district, and one on the southern. But their shrines were remote, the district poor and sparsely inhabited. As a result offerings were very few and far between; in fact, both the deities were near to starvation. One day a boy passed by the shrine of the southern deity, who streched out his hand and touched the boy's body so that when the lad returned home his body began to burn all over and he fell into a high fever. As his family worried over the boy, they heard a voice from the boy's body say that the illness was caused by mountain spirits, that the speaker was the deity of the southern mountain who would cure the ill, and that they should go to his temple, cut off a piece from the camphor tree in front of the shrine and give an infusion made from the wood to the sick boy. The family did as they were instructed and the boy swiftly recovered. To show their gratitude the family sent food and other kinds of offering to the deity who, delighted by the success of his strategy, sent his servant to invite the deity of the northern mountain to have dinner.

His guest was most impressed by the repast and enquired how it had come about. The southern mountain spirit explained in a suitably off-hand manner how he had achieved his success and the deity of the northern mountain resolved to adopt a similar strategy. As luck would have it, his chance occurred the very next day and he was able to touch a passing cowherd. The lad returned home, fell ill and, at once, the deity of the northern mountain entered his body to issue instructions to the stricken family, ordering them to give the sick boy an infusion of camphor wood. The father quickly hurried to the shrine to carry out the deity's orders, but, alas, there was no camphor tree by the northern shrine. He saw the image itself was of camphor wood, but was naturally reluctant to inflict a visible mutiliation upon the image so, lifting its gown, he sliced some wood from the buttocks of the deity. The sick boy was brought back to health, but as the family was unbelievably poor and had nothing for themselves it never occurred to them that it was fitting to offer foodstuffs to the deity. There was no offering at all: the god remained hungry and not unnaturally

The kitchen-god and his consort. He was the most important of the domestic deities, who received offerings twice a month and a special feast of honey at the New Year in order to seal his lips before he went to render his yearly report to Heaven. Paper image designed to be fixed over the kitchen stove. Horniman Museum, London.

wrathful, not least because of the success which his opposite number had achieved with the same gambit. Finally he made his way to the abode of the deity of the southern mountain, where he was received in some surprise. After he had explained his sad circumstances the god of the southern mountain laughed unceasingly and between guffaws said: 'Brother, fancy not remembering that there was no camphor tree by your temple. If one is hurt through one's own stupidity, there is no point in blaming others.'

The Great Wall of China, erected by Shi Huang Di of the Qin dynasty as a protection against attack by the Huns in the north. The large-scale expenditure of resources, the conscription of labour, and the loss of life caused by the rapid building of this vast wall across rugged terrain gave rise to the myth of Meng Jiang Nu, the Pumpkin Girl.

The Heavenly Empire

So far we have been concerned with cosmology and cosmography, with the little that has survived of Chinese ideas about human origins and the creation of living things. But side by side with this mythology there is another system of more direct concern to people in their everyday affairs. If it be true that we create gods in our own image, then the Chinese made a most tidy business of their theogony since the divine world is but a recreation of the earthly bureaucracy on a heavenly scale.

The Supreme Emperor

Imperial China was ruled by the emperor under the protection of Heaven and by the agency of a complex and all-embracing bureaucracy, while Heaven itself was under a supreme sovereign, the August Personage of Jade Yudi. In some traditions Yudi was also the creator of humans, having modelled them in clay; but while they were drying in the sun some got wet: these are the halt and the sick. Yudi dwelt in a palace, just like his earthly counterpart, with a doorkeeper and court functionaries, and had ministers who presided over the various departments concerned with human acitivities. His wife was Wang Mu niang-niang, another form of Xi Wang Mu. It was to this Supreme Emperor that the earthly ruler made the twice-yearly sacrifices at the Altar of Heaven in Peking. These sacrifices ended with the setting up of the Republic in 1912, although they were to persist in Annam, where the court rituals were almost wholly Chinese in manner until the Second World War. The Supreme Emperor was, however, concerned only with the emperor's affairs: it was his ministers who dealt with the problems of lesser mortals.

The Hall of Annual Prayers or Temple of Heaven in Beijing. Its umbrella-like blue-tiled roof is itself symbolic of the circular sky, while its three layers correspond to the Three Heavens. In this temple the Son of Heaven communed with the Supreme Emperor and received his own mandate to rule China.

There were also members of the hierarchy charged with the affairs of such natural phenomena as sun, moon, stars and winds, a system which in many instances diverged quite considerably from that which we have already considered.

Household and Personal Gods

The Supreme Emperor had a doorkeeper for his palace, an armed functionary who served as sentinel and

porter. But the dwelling of every Chinese was similarly protected: indeed each household had a divine as well as a human set of inhabitants. Each of the leaves of the double entrance-door was protected by a separate guardian, while each lesser entrance, to the sides and rear, had a spirit guard for its single leaf. The Lord and Lady of the Bed presided over the bedchamber while the kitchen was the domain of the kitchen-god, whose role was considerably more extensive than his title might suggest. There was even a goddess to preside over the latrines. Inevitably one is reminded of the host of deities which oversaw every aspect of life in pagan Rome from conception to death. And, just as in Rome, so in China there were gods especially charged with the oversight of a man's career, and with the different aspects of a woman's life.

We have no complete list of the ancient gods of China, if ever such a thing existed. Indeed, it is doubtful whether anyone has compiled a complete roll of those who still existed in this century, for there were countless local differences and minor variations. Their origins can be traced to an amalgam of Buddhist and Daoist sources, with elements from much older traditions which contributed to what was in effect a new religion of the people.

In addition to the deities who safeguarded the parts of the house, there was a local deity whose care was the house's situation. Then there was the god of wealth and the three gods of

Above. The three gods of happiness crossing the seas to their Palace of Immortality in the Happy Isles. They are Shoulao, god of long life, Fuxing, god of happiness, and Luxing, god of salaries or of functionaries. All lived on earth as men and by good fortune or merit were deified – which in part explains their popularity. Xi Wang Mu and an attendant follow them. Porcelain dish, reign of Yong Zheng (1723-35). Victoria and Albert Museum, London.

Right. Zai Shen, god of wealth, universally worshipped but especially by poor peasants. He lived on earth as a hermit whose miraculous powers included the ability to ride on the black tiger shown here. He fought for Wu, founder of the Zhou dynasty, against the last of the Shang, Zhou Xin. He was killed by sorcery, but was later immortalised as god of riches. Gilt wood figure. Horniman Museum, London.

Opposite. An ancestress depicted, according to custom, in her marriage robes. The ancestors were the link through which the family approached the gods. The portraits were carefully preserved but brought out only on the first six days of the New Year. More importance was attached to male ancestors, but an ancestress could intercede on behalf of women desiring children. Daoist scroll painting.

happiness: to all these ritual cults were offered at fixed seasons. In the family shrine the ancestral tablets brought to the living generations the spiritual presence of the ancestors, who served as a link with the other world. Each of the deities had an image in front of which incense could be offered. Those of the door-gods and Zao Jun, the god of the kitchen, were of paper, fixed to the door-leaves and above the kitchen stove. For the other gods there were figurines, though in orthodox Confucian families these were frowned upon, a fact which does not seem to have prevented women in such households from having an image of the Buddhist, and therefore heterodox, goddess Guan Yin. In strict Buddhist or Daoist households on the other hand, where figurines and statues were acceptable, the god of literature, Wenchang dadi, had only a tablet inscribed with his title.

Although the pantheon showed such variations, following regional or social distinctions, the whole hierarchy is best seen as a well-organised divine bureaucracy with clearly established grades. These were drawn from Buddhist and Daoist systems as well as from the secular imperial order. Thus we find Buddhas and Bodhisattvas, Arhats, Venerable Celestial Beings, Immortals, Emperors, Empresses, Kings, Gods and Goddesses. Within the system there was a more or less fixed establishment but the individual divinities who filled the specific posts might change, either as their popularity increased or diminished or because of regional variations in cult practices.

Many of the deities were historical or semi-historical figures who became divine because of their terrestrial achievements. These sometimes received promotion within the hierarchy by official, terrestrial decree as in the case of Guan Di which we shall discuss below.

Guan Di, the God of War

Guan Di, in whose honour more than 1,600 official temples, to say nothing of countless minor shrines, were dedicated in Manchu times, was originally

a kind of Robin Hood figure. He was one of three heroes whose adventures are recounted in the *Romance of the Three Kingdoms*, a pseudo-historical account of events at the end of the Later Han dynasty, written at the beginning of the Ming period. Guan Zhong was a native of Shanxi who was forced to flee through the pass to Shaanxi after killing an official for an act of sexual tyranny. There he fell in with a butcher, Zhang Fei, and a peddlar of straw sandals, Liu Bei, who was to be the founder of the Shu Han dynasty of Sichuan. In a peach orchard belonging to Zhang Fei, the three took an oath of loyalty to one another and of service to the state. The story tells of their adventuring and crusading together and the virtues of Guan Zhong until in the end he was captured and executed by one of his opponents, Sun Chuan, in A.D. 219. The virtues of Guan Zhong were later recognised and he was awarded the rank of duke posthumously by an imperial decree in 1120, a rank which was upgraded to that of prince in 1128.

Some years later the Yuan emperor Wen promoted him again to the rank of Warrior Prince and Bringer of Civilisation, which title he held until 1594, when the Ming emperor Wan Li conferred upon the dead hero the title Faithful and Loyal Great Deity (*di*), Supporter of Heaven, Protector of the Realm. During Manchu times his cult reached its peak and it is believed that he appeared in the sky in the support of the imperial forces in 1856. He was adopted as patron of many trades and professions, while the sword of the public executioner was kept in his temple enclosure. Here, after an execution, the supervising magistrate would make offerings so that the spirit of the executed man might not pursue him to his home.

But hero-gods such as Guan Di could also be explained in religious bureaucratic terms. For just as secular bureaucrats were sent into exile from the court, so immortal administrators guilty of some celestial offence might be sent from the heavenly court to spend a period of exile on earth. Then

their military or civil achievements, which were to earn them deification, could be explained as the deeds by which they atoned for their misdemeanours and regained admission to the divine civil service. Only the highest grades, Buddhas, Bodhisattvas and Venerable Celestial Beings, appear to have been exempt from such hazards of advancement and demotion. In their case alone the Buddhist concept of Enlightenment operated (even for the Daoist *tianzun*) and they had reached the point of no return. But they too were conceived of in personal terms, as were

Right. Guan Di with Zhang Fei on his left and Liu Bei on his right. Known as the Three Brothers of the Peach-orchard after the place where they swore friendship, they were renowned for their exploits in upholding justice. Zhang Fei, a butcher, was 8 feet (2.5 metres) tall, with a panther's head, a tiger's beard and round eyes. His voice was like thunder. Eighteenth-century, Daoist scroll painting. Religionskundliche Sammlung der Universität, Marburg.

Below right. The Sixteenth Lohan or Arhat, portrayed as a tormented and repellent ascetic of Indian type. The Arhats formed one of many grades within the divine hierarchy, and were directly derived from Indian and later from Zen Buddhist models. Stone carving in the Lohan Hall at Hangzhou after a painting by the famous monk Guanxiu (832-912).

Above left. Li Tieguai, a pupil of Laozi, who lost his mortal body while his soul was visiting the Master. His soul was reborn into the body of a beggar with an iron crutch. He became one of the Eight Daoist Immortals. Daoist scroll painting. Religionskundliche Sammlung der Universität, Marburg.

Left. An Arhat dreaming. By the exercise of virtue and the practice of contemplation, Arhats, the immediate disciples of Buddha, could attain the reward of a beatific state, which increasingly resembled that of the Daoist Immortals, who lived on dew or on pure jade and floated on the mountain air. Similarly any mortal could by virtue obtain divine aid and better his or her worldly position. Eighteenth-century Buddhist scroll painting. Religionskundliche Sammlung der Universität, Marburg.

Opposite. Guan Yin, goddess of mercy, the female Chinese form of the Bodhisattva Avalokitesvara, who postponed her Buddhahood in order to help the people. Guan Yin was particularly important in northern China. Red amber statuette. Wellcome Institute for the History of Medicine, London.

all the deities of the popular pantheon.

The major deities, it was felt, could not be present at all the many images in their many temples. Such deities were allowed to appoint deputies, the souls of the just, who could act on their behalf, and give account of the ceremonies and rites in the temples to which they were appointed. As compensation they were entitled to receive a proportion of the offerings. Though Chinese popular religion was always concerned above all with personal deities, this is certainly not to say that impersonal forces played no part in Chinese life. Such obscure, powerful and ill-defined forces as Happiness *fu* and Destiny *ming* affected each individual, but these were generally thought of as being within the gift of the individual's personal deities, who might vary each person's share in them as they pleased. Only *feng-shui*, Wind and Water, those mysterious natural forces which influenced sites of buildings, temples,

palaces and tombs as well as those who used or occupied them and what was connected with them, whose powers it was the function of the geomancer to determine, seem to have been conceived of as wholly impersonal and outside the sphere of the gods.

The Sky-god and His Bureaucrats

Who then were these personal deities and what were their functions? Originally, there had been a supreme deity Shang Di who was a sky-god. His function had been to preside over a hierarchy, but his divine nature tended to be eroded by Confucian rationalism and he had become known simply as Tian, Sky. Even in this role, however, he retained his importance, for Sky sees and hears everything: people may whisper but to Sky the sound is as loud as thunder; nothing escapes his eye. Despite the efforts of atheistic scholars, therefore, Sky remained a deity and as such was the supreme figure in the popular pantheon, responsible for individual destiny: each blade of grass has its share of the dew. To him was also attributed the title of the Daoist supreme being, the August of Jade Yuhuang da-di, a title of ancient origin, which received imperial recognition after the deity had appeared twice to Song emperors. There was nothing capricious about Yu-huang's rule: the seaons followed their established plan; *yin* and *yang* were in balance; the good rewarded, the evil punished. But like other supreme deities, Yuhuang became remote and it became more usual to offer ritual to his door-keeper (a reflection no doubt of the necessary preliminaries to obtaining a boon or even justice from a terrestrial functionary). This official, the Transcendent Dignitary, drove off evil spirits from the celestial palace and became a popular figure in the pantheon. Nor did Yu-huang occupy himself any longer with natural phenomena: their charge was assigned to different gods: the Count of the Wind, the Master of the Rain, the

Opposite. Guan Di, god of war, patron of literature, and upholder of justice. He was a popular deity throughout China, not as a wager of war, but as a preventer of strife and protector against evil. War itself was a ritualised system of justice by ordeal. Fujian province. Reign of Kang Xi. Victoria and Albert Museum, London.

Centre. The Eight Daoist Immortals, each of whom was admitted to eternal life as a reward for his acts on earth, bearing gifts to Shoulao, god of long life. As this homage shows, not even the 'Immortals' could be sure of retaining their position at the heavenly court. Porcelain dish, reign of Wan Li (1573-1620). Victoria and Albert Museum, London.

Below. Wine pot in the form of the character *fu*, happiness. Though an abstract force, *fu* was thought to be within the gift of the individual's personal deities. Happiness itself was also personified in the god Fuxing, who was a deified magistrate called Yang Cheng, who saved the people of Hunan from the emperor Wudi's intolerable levy in the sixth century A.D. Victoria and Albert Museum, London.

Opposite. A judge of Hell. Hell, like Heaven, was ruled by an elaborate bureaucracy where the punishments meted out to the evil were exactly calculated to match their crimes. Pottery statue, late Ming. British Museum, London.

Below. Figure of Shoulao, god of long life and originally a stellar deity, who headed one of the seventy-five departments under the jurisdiction of the Great Emperor of the Eastern Peak. It was he who fixed the times of a person's death, inscribing it in his tablets at the moment of birth. Occasionally he was known to change his mind on the entreaty of the parents. He is usually shown smiling. The panels on his robe resemble those of costly silk tapestry and symbolic patterns worn by the courtiers at the imperial court on earth. Reign of Kang Xi. Victoria and Albert Museum, London.

Lord of the Lightning (the celestial executioner who persisted as a living god in popular belief).

Yu-huang's principal aide was Dong-yo da-di, Supreme Ruler of the Eastern Peak, the birthplace of *yang*; he was linked with Dong Wang Gong. As Yu-huang's deputy he was seen as head of a ministry with no fewer than seventy-five departments which were occupied with the supervision of every aspect of life on earth. Here were fixed the times of birth and death, the course of life for all living creatures, as well as an inspectorate responsibile for the oversight of terrestrial deities. Two points are of note. First that human and animal life were equally the concern of Dong-yo da-di's bureaucrats, recruited from amongst the souls of the virtuous dead. Human and animal life formed a continuum because of the Buddhist belief in reincarnation, adopted in its entirety by the Daoists and firmly installed in the popular religion. In this system rebirth as an animal was a typical punishment for an erring human: reincarnation in human form a suitable reward for animal virtue. Another reward or punishment was an increase or reduction of the normal life span: such variations were made at the time of birth by one of the departments in the ministry. The second point is that since all life was the concern of this ministry there were departments specially concerned with such categories as thieves and murderers. So powerful a deity inevitably attracted great popular attention and in Beijing, where his temple at one time had eighty departments, his role as a giver of offspring was recognised by women who sought a son. The ritual was to offer incense and then to take home one of the small dolls deposited as a thank-offering by those whose desire had already been granted. When the wished-for son was born the mother returned the original doll to the temple with a second as her own token of gratitude.

The Gods of the Soil: District Administrators

As we have already seen, the high role attributed to the sky-deity in ancient China was paralleled by a cult of the god of the soil. We should expect that as the cult of the sky-deity continued, though the main cult was now centred about his principal deputy, so would that of the earth-god, though it too perhaps in modified form. And this indeed was the case. The place of the great god of the soil had been taken by a whole series of gods of the wall and moat. This was Cheng-huang, responsible in each district for the land and its inhabitants, who received from local officials the petitions which in earlier, feudal, times had been addressed by rulers to the god of the soil. Cheng-huang was thought to control the ravages of wild beasts or beasts that might destroy the harvest, to break droughts or halt excessive rain and to bring peace and prosperity to the people in his district. At the same time he had some concern with the disposal of the souls of the dead, once Yen-lo, the Buddhist Yama, king of the dead, had summoned the soul to appear before him. Cheng-huang had the right to make sure that Yen-lo's emissaries had acted properly in carrying off that particular one of the inhabitants under his protection. The two servants of the king of the underworld had therefore to present the soul in question at the court of Cheng-huang, who would satisfy himself of the correctness of the summons: that the calculations of the department in Dong-yo da-di's ministry concerned with the length of the creature's days had been properly complied with. He then carried out a preliminary judgment, commiting the soul to the final jurisdiction of Yen-lo.

As we might expect, the district god of wall and moat had his own servants, of whom the best known were Ba lao-ye and Hei lao-ye, Mr White and Mr Black, whose garments matched their titles and whose role was to watch all activities in their town or district by day and by night respectively. And, following a pattern with which we are becoming familiar, each Cheng-huang had a number of subordinate deities, *Tudi zhen* (*zhen* being the title of the lowest grade of divinity), of whom Maspero wrote:

'Each country village, each quarter and each street of a town, each temple, each public building, each bridge, each field has its own; they have their temple, their chapel, their shrine or at least an inscribed tablet according to their importance. In the villages their role is the same as that of Cheng-huang in the towns; they maintain the register of inhabitants and that is why whenever there is a death a group of women from the family concerned goes to announce it to the deity in his temple on the night following the death, weeping and burning gold and silver paper.'

Cheng-huang and the subordinate godlings had no doubt been chthonic deities like the original god of the soil. But during the long period after the cult's appearance and development in the first few centuries of the Christian era they became increasingly anthropomorphised and were generally thought of as district administrators who, after death, had simply been transferred from the terrestrial to the heavenly oversight of the same district, a divine prefect. As a nineteenth-century Chinese viceroy explained, the Cheng-huang actually presided over the administration of a district: he gave happiness to the good and unhappiness to the wicked. He had a special responsibility for those without descendants, who therefore lacked people to make offerings to them. On the occasion of the Seventh Month festival, while the god was taken in procession round his town, the populace made offerings which were treated as being intended for this unfortunate category of spirits.

The Cheng-huang of each place had the rank appropriate to the size and dignity of his charge and was treated as its spiritual magistrate. He was thus frequently consulted by the magistracy in instances where there was difficulty in establishing the truth in a case. He might also be approached by lay people, as happened with the Cheng-huang of Yan Cheng city. An orphan, brought up by his uncle and aunt, was accused of stealing a golden hairpin from the latter.

To prove his innocence the youth went to swear an oath before the image of Cheng-huang. As he left the temple he stumbled and fell, precisely the fate he had invoked should he have been guilty of the theft. He was therefore driven out by his relations. By virtue and industry, however, he achieved success and became a mandarin. Returning to his old home, he went back to the temple and slept there, the standard method of consulting the god, in order to seek out the truth of the matter. In a dream he learnt that the pin was, in fact, under the floorboards in his relatives' house. It was duly discovered, and the young mandarin went back to the temple to offer thanks and reproaches to Cheng-huang for finally revealing the truth. 'You caused me to fall,' he said, 'so that people believed in my guilt. Now you accept my offerings. Are you not ashamed? You have no face!' At these words the plaster from the face of the image fell to the floor and despite attempts to repair it, the statue remained faceless from then on. Of course, people tried to excuse the deity, saying that he had been away from the temple on the day that the orphan first approached him, and that the minor spirits had caused the boy to stumble out of malice. But it was curious that it was not possible to restore his face.

Guardians of the Home

Dong-yo da-di and Cheng-huang were concerned with human and animal destiny and how the destined existence was carried out. But the detailed control and manipulation of this was in the hands of a multiplicity of other deities. As we have already noted the house itself was the province of a number of separate specialists of whom the most important, without any doubt, was the kitchen-god. He seems to have been originally a Daoist deity and has been described as the Chief of the Secret Police to the Daoist supreme being. Offerings were made to his paper representation twice a month, at the new and the full moon, and he was the object of special attentions before the New Year when he went to Heaven to render his report of the family whose most intimate observer he was in fact believed to be.

According to legend his cult developed in Han times. A certain Daoist priest called Li Shao-zhun obtained from him the double boon of perpetual youth and freedom from the need for food. The priest then went to the emperor Wudi (141-87 B.C.) and promised him all kinds of benefit, including those alchemical secrets which it was believed the mythical emperor Huang Di had possessed, if the cult of the kitchen-god under the direction of Li Shao-zhun were to receive imperial patronage and support. After the priest had succeeded in contriving an appearance of the god before the emperor, the latter made a sacrifice to him, fully persuaded that he too would receive the pill which granted immortality and the secret of making gold. When the expected rewards failed to materialise, the emperor grew sceptical and the frantic priest sought to contrive another miracle like that of the god's manifestation. He therefore caused an ox to swallow a piece of silk on which he had written a few phrases. He then predicted that if the ox were to be slain, magical writings would be found in its stomach. Everything turned out as the priest had predicted, but unfortunately the emperor recognised the writing as that of Li Shao-zhun and ordered his execution. Since the god was already installed in favour, however, his cult continued to flourish despite his patron's ignominious end.

The kitchen-god was not one of the original five genii of the house, to whom sacrifices were made. It is likely, however, that his cult was already established in ancient times, though not yet in its developed and popular style. The earliest domestic gods were the god of the interior courtyard, who served as the god of the soil for the house, the smallest territorial unit; the god of the entrance door, of the back door, of the aisles (the traditional house had a number of aisles under a single roof); and the god of the well. In post-Han times the importance of these various deities changed considerably and the kitchen-god, indisputably the most important of them, was thought of as their chief and leader. Next in standing were the *men shen*, two deities to be seen, one each, on the leaves of the front door, where their vividly coloured images were attached. In popular belief one of them was good, the other evil, although in their later forms they were officially supposed to be two translated generals Yu Zhe and Qin Shu-bao, who heroically defended the gates of the imperial palace against demonic assault in Tang China. Fully accoutred and armed with halberds, they barred the entrance to the house against all evil spirits and against demons bringing pestilence. The back door was guarded by yet another deity.

The story goes that the emperor Dai Zong (A.D. 627-50) lay sick in his palace and thought that he heard demons prowling in his bedroom. He had tried unsuccessfully to obtain a reprieve for a dragon which had distributed rain erroneously, a fault for which he had been sentenced to decapitation by the August Personage of Jade. The dragon was haunting him in reproach. When he informed the empress and the doctors who were called to treat him of this, saying that even when the days were peaceful, the nights were full of demonic assaults, they were much concerned and the two heroes volunteered to defend the door of the imperial bedchamber at night. Their watch was successful and the night passed without disturbance. They continued their vigil for subsequent nights until the emperor, anxious for their well-being, ordered them to desist, but, for safety's sake, to paint their portraits, in full panoply, upon the leaves of the door. These substitute sentinels were effective for a number of nights, but then similar demonic assaults began through the back entrance to the palace. Thereupon the minister Wei Cheng offered to guard the rear gate in the same manner as Qin Shu-bao and Yu Zhe had guarded the front. The effort was successful and thenceforward Dai Zong's nights were undisturbed. As a result the brightly painted figures of the *men shen*, renewed each New Year, at a time when all the household deities received special attention, were to be seen on every door.

This heroic pair were not, however, the original guardians of the entrance. They were replacements for an earlier couple, Shen Shu and Yu Lei. Once, many millennia ago, an immense peach tree grew on Mount Tu Shuo in the Eastern Sea. Its branches covered many acres, and the lowest of these, which inclined towards the north-east, served as a doorway for devils (*gueï*). There were two spirits stationed by the branch bridge to seize those demons which had harmed men and hand them over to were-tigers for destruction. Huang Di had pictures of the two spirits painted on peachwood and hung above doors to keep off demons. Gradually the custom grew of depicting Shen Shu and Yu Lei, armed with bow and arrows and spears, the one on the left, the other on the right of doors. These figures, like those of later times, were painted on paper stuck on the leaves of the doors.

Demon Spirits

These *guei* were one category among a number of beings harmful to human beings. The souls of those who met death by drowning or who commited suicide, and were thus unable to attain a further incarnation, were forced to return as dangerous ghosts to earth. The drowned were freed from their wanderings and returned to the normal reincarnation cycle when the death of another mortal at the site of their own drowning liberated them. Suicides seem never to have been able to escape from the special town to which all suicides were consigned. It was generally believed that these ghosts were bound

Fairy with a basket. Though many fairies were benefactors of mankind, men had to treat them warily, for spirits of evil intent masquerading as beautiful women seduced men and so redeemed themselves at their victims' expense. Ivory. Národní Galerie, Prague.

Above. Brass handle in the shape of a dragon-headed door-guardian. Dragons were normally beneficent but in some forms, like the *taotie*, could be frightening. From a Mongolian temple door. Museum of Religion, Ulan Bator, Mongolia.

Opposite. One of the *men shen*, door-guardians, deified generals of the Tang dynasty. Armed with halberds, arrows and magic symbols, they guarded the house against evil spirits and pestilence. Such paper images of the *men shen* were pasted to the door during the New Year celebrations. Painting from Suzhou, nineteenth century.

to wander because their sudden and violent deaths meant that they had not completed the life-cycle assigned to them by the bureaucrats of Dong-yo da-di. In consequence they had to live out the balance of their given days as ghosts until they were permitted to enter limbo and be reborn.

The *guei* were not alone, however. There were many other maleficent creatures, some of which were animals who, as they grew old, developed the power to transform themselves into human forms. Of these the best-known were the foxes who became beautiful young men and women, seduced the opposite sex and then slowly consumed their being in order to prolong their own lives. Such beasts were believed to survive for eight hundred or a thousand years at the expense of a succession of victims.

The emperor Yu was said, as we have seen, to have observed a white fox as an auspicious omen when seeking for a bride, but in general the beast was considered inauspicious and evil. This was in part because it lies up by day and moves at night, thereby receiving an excess of the dark, inferior female half of the *yin-yang* entity. On the other hand it is this avoidance of the light which, according to some sources, was responsible for the asserted longevity of the fox, a characteristic which in this view it shares with other nocturnal creatures such as badgers (also ill-omened and often confused with the fox in legends) and moles. The flesh of the fox was most important in the Chinese traditional pharmacopaeia despite (or perhaps because of) the creature's ill-repute. Its entrails too had their medicinal values, while the saliva of the fox 'gathered in a decoy-jar with a narrow neck and having a bait inside, is given as a love-potion to cold wives'. Further the fox was thought to have a mysterious power to make fire, either by banging its brush upon the ground or by emitting a fire-ball from its mouth. As a creature often found inhabiting crevices in ancient tombs, it was easy enough for the fox to become associated with the spirits of the dead, whose wrongs it was thought to avenge against the living who had been responsible for them. But the fox itself, possessor of a power to foresee the future and thus its own death, was also the epitome of a seemly death. 'The fox died correctly with his head on the mound' is a phrase used to describe such a proper death and refers to an ancient belief.

There were other demon animals and even objects which had to be viewed with extreme circumspection. The danger was always when the

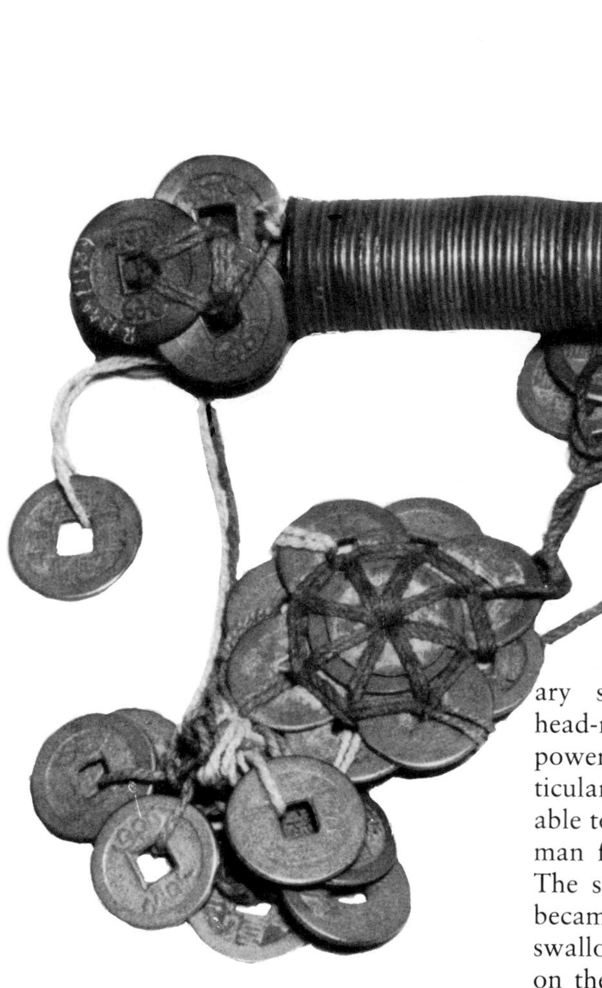

object in question was old, and more especially if it had human associations over a long period of time. The statues of horses before the ancient tombs of high officials could journey at night and even take human form. The mounds which supported funerary steles, like ancient porcelain head-rests, were possessed of sinister powers, as were ancient trees or particular stones. Some of these too were able to transform themselves into human form and prey upon mankind. The souls of people eaten by tigers became bond slaves to the beasts that swallowed them and hunted others on their behalf. They hoped thereby to gain their own release, for having died violently they were *guei* and removed from the cycle of reincarnation until they could find another soul to take their place.

Fearsome though these demons might be, the Men Shen were usually capable of repelling them. The kitchen-god and others of the household deities could dispose of most of those who passed the guardians of the doors, especially if they were supported by amulets and charms strategically disposed about the house – some of general protective intention, some specific for certain evil spirits. Further defences were available in the strategic situation of the house at the end of a street or beside a bridge, since spirits were reluctant to cross flowing water. A brick screen before the entrance, or a simple single stone would serve to deter many of the demons, who were apparently bound to travel in straight lines. A net suspended about the cradle or the smoke from burning slippers would protect the infant during its first hundred days from the attack of *touziguei*, young women who died before marriage and were therefore eager to steal babies in place of those of whom they had been deprived.

Left. Door-ring holder in the shape of a monstrous tiger head. The tiger was able to repel demons over which the domestic gods had no power, and his protection was particularly required on the fifth day of the fifth month. Six Dynasties period (A.D. 479-581). Cleveland Museum of Art, Ohio. Purchase from the J. H. Wade Fund.

Above. Sword made of coins threaded with string and hung on the curtains of a cot to protect newborn babies from the *touzi guei*, the spirits of women who had died without children and who tried to steal infants. Wellcome Institute for the History of Medicine, London.

Opposite. Deity of fearsome aspect, whose task was to repel demons attempting to approach the house. Several lines of defence against demons were placed round each house. Stoneware roof tile of the Ming dynasty. Perret-Vibert Collection.

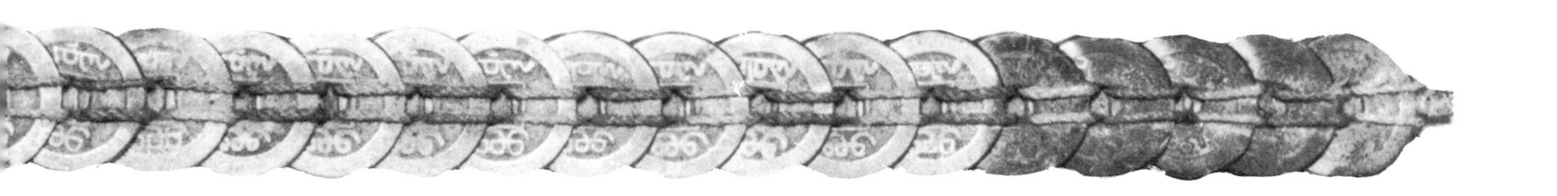

Astrologers and other specialists of the horoscope were able, by their calculations, to warn of especially dangerous days and periods in the life of the young when precautions against demonic attack were particularly necessary. Should such precautions fail, then Daoist exorcists would perform their rituals to expel the maleficent spirits and exorcise the victim. For those who voyaged outside the protection of the domestic deities, there were calendars which listed the days of great risk, the worst being the fifth of the fifth month, when drawings of tigers (in their apotropaic or deterrent role) were fixed to doors and walls, and the character tiger written upon the foreheads of young children. On such perilous days, the prudent person stayed at home and avoided new enterprises.

Horse on the processional way to a Han tomb near Xian. Popular tradition holds that such animals came to life at night and might even assume human form. Were-creatures, especially foxes, play a significant part in Chinese legends. They were generally malevolent, though stories of kindness to humans are not unknown. It seems likely that the Japanese tradition of were-foxes was of Chinese origin.

Humans and Animals

There are many other stories which deal with relations between humans and animals. These serve various ends. One, for instance, explains why monkeys have red-ringed eyes and naked buttocks. These characteristics are the result of devices used by a human bride to elude her monkey husband, aided by her mother. The husband, like the forsaken merman, is left weeping and crying: 'Monkey wife, monkey wife, it is unnatural to abandon your children. They are in tears and your husband mourns.'

How the Oxen Twisted Their Horns

There are many myths about oxen. One rather charming one from Yunnan sets out to explain why it is that some cattle have twisted horns.

There was once a Thai girl who, being thirsty, drank from a mountain stream. And as she drank she noticed a vegetable root drifting in the water, whose leaves had been nibbled by some animal, but whose flesh remained whole and unharmed. She therefore peeled it and ate the inside, which was both sweet and thirst-quenching. Afterwards she became pregnant and gave birth to a baby girl. The people were pleased, for the child was sweet-voiced and a beautiful dancer. All the men, both young and old, fell victims to her beauty; but when the young men learnt that

The ox was originally a star-deity, but through his own stupidity he was forced to remain on earth to help farmers with their ploughing. He bore no grudge, however. Many, such as the father of the Thai girl and his companions, were regarded as holy animals, especially under Indian influence. Seventeenth-century jade, Ming dynasty. Victoria and Albert Museum, London.

she had no father they could no longer risk being seen in her company, while the women cursed her as being begotten out of marriage.

The child grew unhappy and asked her mother why she did not have a father as other children did. Finally, her mother told her the story of her conception, adding that she was certain that even if her daugher were to see her father, she would be sure to dislike him, for he was bound to be very ugly. But the child insisted that, even if ugly, the man would still be her father. So then the mother revealed that the child's father was in fact a holy ox, who had told her in a dream on the day of the child's birth that it was he who had eaten the leaves of the vegetable, and that he dwelt in the midst of the mountains. The child asked why her mother had made no attempt to find the ox, and the mother explained that she did not feel able to leave her child among the hostile villagers while she went on such a search. So the child resolved to go herself in search of her father and asked her mother how she would recognise him. 'Take roots with you, my child, and feed them to the oxen that you meet upon your way in the mountains. When you find an ox that eats only the leaves, that will be your father.'

The next morning the child set off into the mountains and searched until she found, deep in the mountains, an ox which ate only the leaves of the proferred root. She followed him till she came to a cave where he lived with many other magic oxen. Near the cave she found a hollow tree in which to live. In the mornings she cleaned out the cave where the cattle dwelt, and when they returned in the evening they were astonished to find the cave cleared of dung. This continued until one day the ox who was her father stayed behind and discovered that it was the girl who was cleaning out the cave in which they dwelt. Then he recognised his daughter.

The girl continued to live in the hollow tree until the autumn, when it began to grow cold. But despite her father's entreaties she would not return to her village, preferring to die of cold in the mountains to returning to the hostile villagers. Her father therefore determined to build her a home. The only building material he had was horn, so all the cattle took off their horns and gave them to the girl's father to build her a house of horn. It was quickly done and soon, when only one more horn was required to complete the very beautiful building, the father ox called out 'enough'. Then those of the magic cattle who were still twisting their horns in order to take them off stopped. And that is why the horns of some cattle are straight while those of others are twisted.

The Dog who Married a Princess

But of marriages with animals the best-known tale is probably that which tells how a dog married the daughter of the Emperor of China.

The Emperor was engaged in war against a neighbouring ruler to the west. His army was so badly defeated that his generals were reluctant to continue the struggle. In the end, to embolden them, the Emperor was forced to issue a proclamation offering his daughter in marriage to the warrior who should bring him the head of the enemy chief. The proclamation was much discussed in the Chinese camp, but though the Emperor's daughter was a worthy reward in every way no one could be found bold enough to undertake the enterprise.

A large dog belonging to one of the generals heard the talk and, slipping quietly out of the camp, made his way through the enemy lines into the tent of the chief. Here he gnawed off the head of the enemy chief and returned with it to his own camp, where he laid it at the feet of the Emperor. The enemy were seen to be in confusion and soon withdrew to the rejoicing of the victorious Chinese. At this point the dog reminded the Emperor of his promise. The latter explained the impossibility of a marriage between the

dog and an imperial princess, whereupon the dog proposed that he should transform himself into a man by being placed under a bell, removed from human eyes, for the space of 280 days. The emperor agreed to the proposal and for 279 days the dog remained undisturbed inside the bell. But on the two hundred and eightieth day the emperor was unable to restrain his curiosity any longer and, lifting the rim, he peeped underneath.

The dog was wholly transformed save only for his head. The spell having been broken by the Emperor's rash action, however, his daughter was now faced with a dog-headed suitor. Since the fault was entirely the Emperor's, the marriage had to take place, though the bridegroom's head was carefully covered with a red cloth for the occasion. (Some stories say that it was the bride who was veiled in red so that she might not see her husband's ugly head.) The children were fair of limb but unfortunately had their father's head. To this day, therefore, the tribesmen known as the Rong of Fuzhou wear a red head-covering to disguise their features. These people still paint a dog on a screen at the time of the old-style New Year and make offerings to it, saying that it is a representation of their ancestor who defeated the enemy from the west.

The Farmer who Befriended a Fox

Though many encounters with foxes were disastrous, from time to time we come across stories where the fox, pleased with its treatment, brings wealth and success to the host who has befriended it. But then friendship has its hazards.

Opposite left. Bronze support in the form of a tiger. Late Zhou period (fifth to third centuries B.C.). Seattle Art Museum, Washington. Eugene Fuller Memorial Collection.

Centre. Porcelain plate depicting a carp attempting to leap the Longmen Falls or Dragon Gate on the Yellow River at the border between Shaanxi and Shanxi provinces. Once a year all the fish competed in this attempt, those which succeeded being transformed immediately into dragons and rising up into the sky. Dragons are said to rise to the skies in spring and to plunge into the waters in autumn. Reign of Kang Xi. Victoria and Albert Museum, London.

Below. A pair of cranes which may have served as an incense burner. Cranes were symbolic of happiness and also of literary elegance, so that they were appropriate images both of Fuxing and of Wenchang, god of literature. Národní Galerie, Prague.

Left. Imperial Dragons and the Flaming Pearl, which represents the sun. The pearl guarded by the dragon in the water represents imperial treasure. Like the Indian Nagarajas, the Dragon Kings kept their treasures in fabulous underwater palaces made of crystal and they fed upon pearls and opals. There were five of them, corresponding to the Five Mountains, and once a year they all rose out of the waters and without wings flew up to Heaven to report to the Supreme Emperor. Kesi silk tapestry panel, Ming dynasty (1368-1644). Seattle Art Museum, Washington. Eugene Fuller Memorial Fund.

Opposite. Zhongguei, god of examinations. Having been denied the first place in the examinations which he had won, he committed suicide and so became *guei.* He was worshipped by travellers as a protector against the evil spirits who haunt roads. One of these red-haired demons stands behind him. Screen painting, nineteenth century. Victoria and Albert Museum, London.

There was once a man with an enormous straw stack. As straw was removed, a hole was left in which a fox took up its home. It used to appear to the owner of the stack in the form of an old man, a favourite transformation of foxes. One day it invited the owner to visit it in its hole, which turned out to contain a long set of handsomely furnished apartments. Here superb tea and fine wines were served. The fox was wont to spend the nights away from the straw yard and admitted that he went to take wine with friends. The owner begged to be allowed to accompany him and to this the fox agreed, though with reluctance. So they set off through the air until, in the time it takes to cook a pot of millet, they reached a city where they entered a restaurant in which a great company was drinking. They went into the gallery, to which the fox brought wine and various delicacies. Then a handsomely dressed man brought a dish of preserved cumquats to a table below. The owner asked the fox to fetch some, but the latter admitted that he could not do so since he who had brought them was an upright man whom a fox might not approach. His guest reflected that in frequenting the company of the fox he had lost the right to be considered upright and resolved that henceforward he would follow a path of probity. As he pondered, he fell from the gallery into the company below and the fox disappeared. Looking up he saw that there was no gallery, only a large rafter on which he must have been sitting. The astonished company listened to his account of his adventure and then collected money to pay for his return home, for he was a thousand *li* from his house and straw yard.

Monkey

Of the purely animal stories, that of Monkey is certainly the best known. The manner in which the monkey became part of the Chinese pantheon is told in the *Xi yu ji*, an account of a journey to the Western Paradise in order to obtain the Buddhist scriptures for the Emperor of China. The story is, in fact, a version of the true story of the introduction of Buddhism into China. It tells of Tang Seng, a pilgrim (the historical Xuan Zang), who went to India, the land of the Buddha, to obtain true texts of the Buddha's teachings, and died in A.D. 664. Tang Seng was accompanied on his journey by the Monkey Fairy, Sun houzi, who like human beings was prone to evil, and Chu Bajie, a Pig-spirit representing the coarser elements in the human spirit.

Monkey was born from an egg which had been fertilised by the wind as it lay on the peak of a mountain in Ao-lai on the eastern side of the Ocean. He became unbelievably adept at magic arts and learnt further skills from a Daoist Immortal who among other things gave him the personal name of Discoverer of Secrets, taught him to change his shape at will and to fly through the air. Monkey organised all the monkeys of the world into a kingdom and slew a monster who was persecuting them. He obtained a magic weapon from the Dragon King of the Eastern Sea with which he began to make himself master of the four quarters.

Then, at a great feast given in his honour, Monkey drank too much; while he was asleep he was seized by the servants of the king of Hell, who had him chained in the infernal regions. He broke his bonds, however, and stole the register of judgments from which he deleted his own name and that of all monkeys. As a result of all the trouble which he caused he was summoned to Heaven to explain

北京周培春

his conduct. The Lord of Heaven made him Grand Overseer of the Heavenly Stables to keep him quiet. This succeeded until Monkey learnt of the true reasons for his appointment, started to break up Heaven itself and then withdrew to Mount Huaguo. The Heavenly Host organised a siege of the mountain, but was repulsed. Finally, after Monkey had proclaimed himself Governor of Heaven and Great Saint, terms were arranged and he agreed to conform to the divine laws as Superintendent in Chief of the Heavenly Peach Garden, the source of Immortality. Unfortunately he was not invited to the Peach Festival and thus to revenge himself he not only ate all the food and wine prepared for the feast but stole the pills of immortality from the house of Lao Zhun. As Monkey had already eaten the peaches he was thus made doubly immortal. After this he retired once again to Mount Huaguo. But his irresponsible behaviour had by now infuriated all the gods and

Left. The reception of the Immortals at the court of Xi Wang Mu in preparation for the Peach Festival, which was held on the goddess's birthday every three thousand years. When Monkey stole the entire feast, the Jade Emperor decided that he was beyond redemption and must be condemned to death. Scroll painting. British Museum, London.

Opposite. Laozi, the first teacher of Daoism, who resided in the Daoist Third Heaven. In his popular form as Laojun he was a powerful sorcerer. His intervention led to the capture of Monkey, but not even his furnace could prevail against Monkey's double protection of immortality. Daoist scroll painting. Religionskundliche Sammlung der Universität, Marburg.

Below. Monkey vases. Several myths centre on monkeys and their relations with human beings. They were subject to the same hardships and frailties as humans; the Monkey Fairy Sun, *hou-tzu*, who represented human nature and its propensity to evil, was popular for getting away with it and vindicating his nature by his services on the journey to the Western Paradise. Porcelain, *famille rose*, reign of Qian Long.

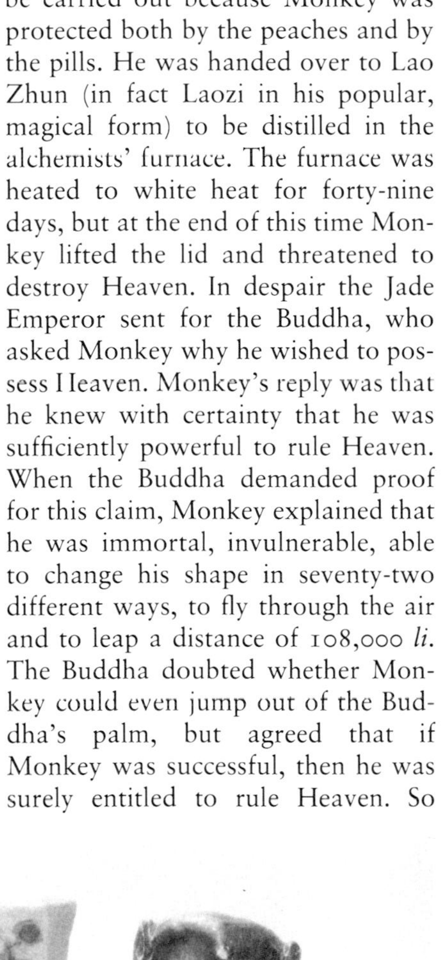

goddesses. After a long siege in which Monkey employed all his magic skills to avoid defeat, he was finally captured and brought before the Jade Emperor, who condemned him to death as a base criminal in revolt against the Heavenly Throne.

The sentence could not, however, be carried out because Monkey was protected both by the peaches and by the pills. He was handed over to Lao Zhun (in fact Laozi in his popular, magical form) to be distilled in the alchemists' furnace. The furnace was heated to white heat for forty-nine days, but at the end of this time Monkey lifted the lid and threatened to destroy Heaven. In despair the Jade Emperor sent for the Buddha, who asked Monkey why he wished to possess Heaven. Monkey's reply was that he knew with certainty that he was sufficiently powerful to rule Heaven. When the Buddha demanded proof for this claim, Monkey explained that he was immortal, invulnerable, able to change his shape in seventy-two different ways, to fly through the air and to leap a distance of 108,000 *li*. The Buddha doubted whether Monkey could even jump out of the Buddha's palm, but agreed that if Monkey was successful, then he was surely entitled to rule Heaven. So Monkey leaped into the air and sprang prodigiously across Heaven to the furthest confines of the earth, where he came to rest at the base of a great mountain. Here he pissed as animals do when they wish to mark out a territory as their own. Then he returned in a single bound and confronted the Buddha. (In the more respectable texts it is said that like a genteel tourist Monkey wrote his name on one of the rocks.) But the Buddha laughed at his claim to have traversed the whole universe at a single bound and showed him that the mountain where he had pissed was but the base of one of the Buddha's fingers and that he had not even

escaped from the palm of the Buddha's hand. Then the Buddha created a magic mountain and shut Monkey within it.

Here he would have remained for ever had the Bodhisattva Guan Yin not obtained his release so that he might accompany Tang Seng on his great pilgrimage to the Western Paradise to fetch authentic versions of the Buddha's teachings. The Monkey swore faithfully to obey his new master and to protect him from perils: this he did despite many temptations upon the way and some eighty mighty perils which the pilgrims had to undergo. On their return a last hazard awaited them when a turtle, who was conveying them and the scriptures across a flooded river, finding that Tang Seng had not yet fulfilled a vow he had made to the turtle on their outward journey, swam away and left them to sink. But they swam safely ashore and were greeted with great honours by the Emperor and the people.

Their final honours came from a heavenly committee of welcome under the presidency of Mi-luo Bodhisattva (the Buddha yet to come). Tang Seng was recognised as a former chief disciple of the Buddha and granted a high rank in Heaven. Monkey was made God of Victorious Strife, and the Pig was created Chief Divine Altar Cleanser. The horse who had carried Tang Seng and the scriptures was turned into a four-clawed dragon and chief of celestial dragons. Now, at the beginning of his pilgrimage Tang Seng had fitted on Monkey a helmet which contracted upon his skull when he was wayward or wanton. The agony of the contractions had caused him to refrain from wickedness. When, therefore, he was given his new title, Monkey begged Tang Seng to remove the helmet, since he had now become an enlightened one. Tang Seng answered that if Monkey was indeed enlightened, the helmet would have gone of its own accord. Monkey reached up to feel his head and found the helmet had disappeared.

The Miraculous Qilin

It seems that in the oldest Chinese tradition the ritualised concept of war was that of justice by ordeal. There was an initial offering of blood, which might perhaps be used to anoint a war-drum; the combat itself was construed as a stylised encounter. On its termination the prisoners were brought to justice at a formal trial in a ceremonial hall and those of double heart were condemned.

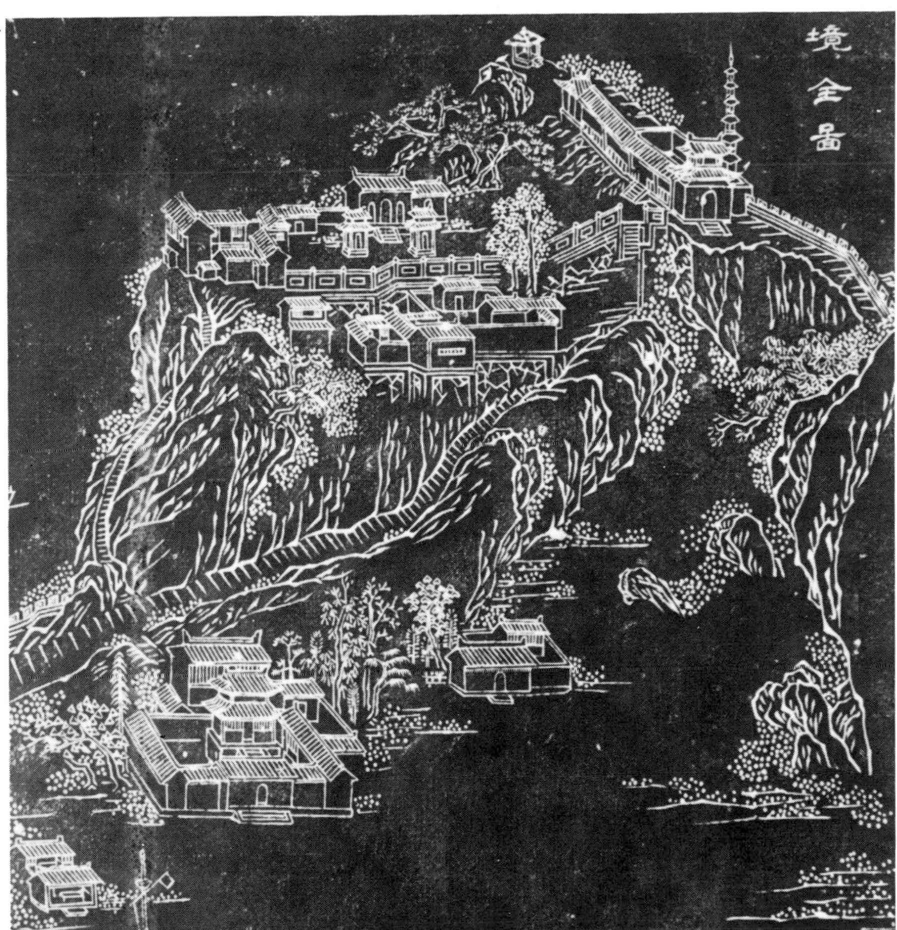

Left. The Four Kings of Hell, who correspond to the Four Diamond Kings of Heaven in Buddhist belief. Other systems held that there were ten hells, or even fourteen – each with its own king but under the control of Yen-lo. They guarded the register of judgments which Monkey stole. In the Six Dynasties period (A.D. 479–581) popular belief assimilated the Buddhist kings with the *fangxiang*, an ancient deity who warded off evil spirits and illness. Four such figures, in armour, might be placed in a tomb in a protective role, either to protect the living or the dead. A similar role was played by a *qitou*, a grotesque being created, according to a Han text, to keep the dead from roaming free. Anonymous painting. British Museum, London.

Above. Jin Shan, the Buddhist island of gold, on which stood a famous monastery. When Tang Seng was born, his mother was at the mercy of her husband's murderer; on the advice of Guan Yin she cast the infant on the waves, and he was later washed up on Jin Shan and brought up by the monks. Buddhist scroll painting. Religionskundliche Sammlung der Universität, Marburg.

Gaoyao, the judge of Shun, the last of the Five Emperors and predecessor of Yu, was considered to be the embodiment and exemplar of this justice. The emblem of Gaoyao was the *qilin*, an auspicious creature. Its body was that of a deer, with the tail of an ox, horse's hooves and a single, fleshy horn. The hair on its back was varicoloured, that on its belly yellow. When it walked it did not crush the grass and it consumed no living creature. It spared the innocent but struck the guilty with its single horn, its action being determined by the findings of the upright judge Gaoyao. In another version Gaoyao's judgments were executed by a single-horned

Opposite left. Buddha riding on a dragon. The horse who had carried Tang Seng on his great pilgrimage to the Western Paradise and had faithfully borne back the authentic versions of the Buddha's teachings to China was rewarded by being made into a dragon, and chief of the celestial dragons who guard the mansions of the gods. Buddhist scroll painting, *c.* seventeenth to eighteenth century A.D. Religionskundliche Sammlung der Universität, Marburg.

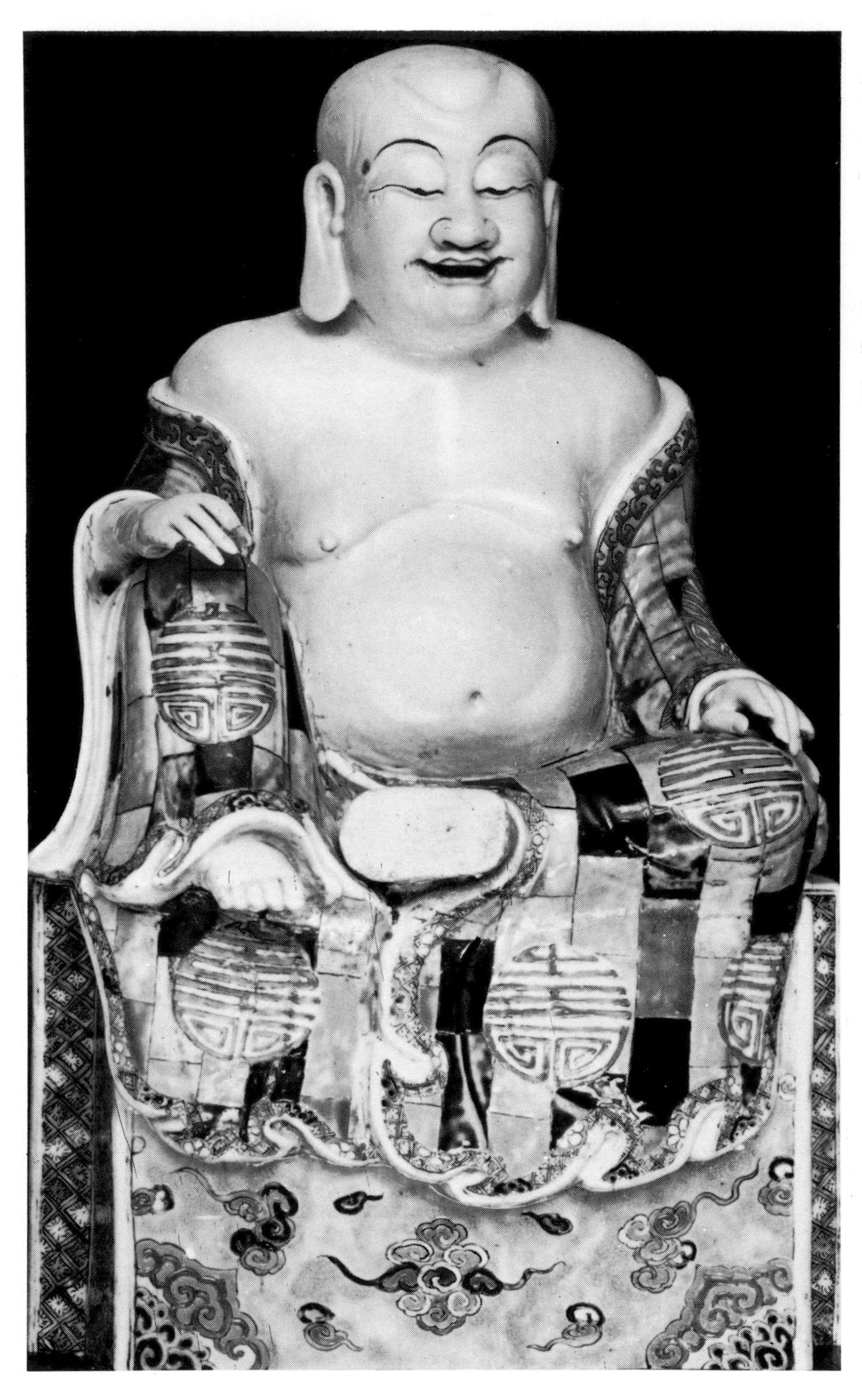

ram, a story which, it has been suggested, derives from some type of trial by ordeal involving the offering of such an animal and swearing by its blood.

When the judgments of a prince achieved ideal justice, a *qilin* was born in his court, attracted thither by the beneficent virtue of the prince. The appearance at the imperial court of miraculous beasts was a proof of the favour of Heaven and of the emperor's supreme virtue, for it was only when the cosmic order had achieved a perfect balance that there was a sufficient amount of cosmic force to allow the production of such wonders.

Such an occasion arose during the Ming dynasty, in the reign of the emperor Yung Lo, the third of the Ming line. The whole story is a curious one, for it is involved with the voyages of exploration by the Jewel Ships, under the command of the Three Jewel Eunuch, Zheng Ho, a Muslim from Yunnan, who led the Ming fleet to the coast of Africa in the early fifteenth century. The expeditions were inspired by the appearance in the capital of a giraffe, sent as tribute from Bengal, where it had been imported from Africa. Now the collection of exotic beasts had long been a feature of the imperial capital and, during the voyages which the Ming fleet undertook, it had been part of their duties to collect the rare, the strange, the exotic for adding to the imperial treasure. For reasons both complicated and obscure it seems that the professional courtiers, the eunuchs who surrounded the Ming court, contrived that a giraffe should be presented to their ruler. By a curious coincidence the Somali name for giraffe is *girin*, a word which to a Ming Chinese would sound most auspiciously like *qilin*, the name of the emblem of justice, embodiment of princely virtue as expressed in the giving of judgment. Physically, too, the giraffe had points of resemblance to the *qilin* with its deer-like body,

Above. This wooden unicorn from Wuwei, Gansu, dates from the Later (Eastern) Han period. It is assumed to be a Han attempt to represent a *qilin*, a highly auspicious animal. The texts generally agree that such a beast had a deer's body, with the tail of a cow and the hoofs of a horse. It was noted for its benevolence, though its horn was a powerful weapon against evil-doers.

Right. Guardian lion of the Sui or early Tang dynasty, c. A.D. 600. Some of the most common animal figures in Chinese art fall into the category of miraculous beasts whose presence proved the favour of Heaven. Lions were not native to China, and were treated as fantastic animals, often used to guard tombs. The first examples are Han (second century A.D.). They were much used for four centuries thereafter, lined up in pairs along the Spirit Road to the south of the tomb. Cleveland Museum of Art, Ohio. Purchase from the J. H. Wade Fund.

Opposite. Miluo Fo, otherwise known as Maitreya or the 'laughing Buddha', under whose presidency a heavenly committee welcomed Monkey and Tang Seng back from their successful pilgrimage. Images of the pot-bellied Miluo Fo, who was identified with the god of wealth, were common at the entrance to temples. Porcelain. Victoria and Albert Museum, London.

七殿泰山王

Above. The *qilin*, a fabulous creature of good omen which was the emblem of the upright judge Gaoyao, and which spared the innocent but struck the guilty with its single horn. Detail from an early nineteenth-century chair cover. Victoria and Albert Museum, London.

Opposite. The Seventh Hell, which was the place of punishment for desecrators of graves and eaters and sellers of human flesh. The Yama, King of the Seventh Hell, dressed like an emperor and surrounded by ministers or court officials, is receiving offerings from supplicants while he watches a dog and devils with flails chasing condemned souls into a river. Fourteenth-century painting. Horniman Museum, London.

oxtail, hooves, horn, variegated hide with yellow underparts, eating no flesh and of a gentle disposition.

When the giraffe arrived from Bengal there was much excitement at the Ming court, and the Board of Rites expressed a desire to present to the emperor a congratulatory memorial. This was declined by the emperor, who expressed the view that if the ministers exerted themselves for the exercise of good government, then if the world was at peace, there was no hindrance to good rule even without a *qilin*. This was in September 1414. In the following year a second giraffe, procured, it seems most likely, by the court eunuchs, arrived at the court. Once again the emperor declined to receive a memorial of congratulations, but he did proceed in state to the Perfumed Gate to receive a zebra, an oryx and the giraffe in the presence of his prostrated ministers and officials. He attributed the arrival of the auspicious creatures to the abundance of virtue which had accrued to his father the previous emperor and, he added graciously, to the assistance which he had received from his ministers. To this was also to be attributed the constant influx of foreign visitors (all of whom tended, in accordance with a tradition of considerable antiquity, to be treated as coming to China in token of their country's recognition of Chinese suzerainty).

But while the emperor was modestly disclaiming any part in the reappearance of the *qilin*, and indeed inviting his ministers to remonstrate with him over any shortcomings that they might detect in his exercise of the heavenly mandate, others had no doubt of the true reasons for the auspicious manifestation. Painters recorded the miraculous beast and the poet Shen Du of the Imperial Academy offered an ode explaining that 'when a sage possesses virtue of extreme benevolence so as to illumine the darkest places, a *qilin* appears'. Such an appearance was clear proof that His Majesty's virtue equalled that of Heaven, whose mercy and blessing had been distributed so universally that its harmonious emanations had produced a *qilin* as unending bliss for the state for a myriad, myriad years. Therefore, continued the poet:

I, your servant, joining the multitude, regard respectfully this auspicious omen and, kneeling a hundred times and knocking my head upon the ground, I present the following hymn of praise:

How glorious is the Sacred Emperor whose literary and military virtues are most excellent,
Who has succeeded to the Precious Throne and has achieved Perfect Order in imitation of the Ancients!
Tranquillity prevails throughout the myriad countries and the Three Luminaries follow their due course;
The Hot and the Rainy Seasons occur in due order and each year sees the harvesting of rice and millet;
The people rejoice in their customs without rift or impediment:
In consequence, auspicious manifestations have occurred universally.
A Zouyu [vegetarian tiger] *has indeed appeared; springs of flavourful water and sweet dew have issued forth.*
Miraculous ears have occurred plentifully: the River has run clear.
The occurrence of all the Happinesses is a true token of Heaven's aid,
A true token of Heaven's aid and a proclamation of Heaven's favour.
Now in the twelfth year, in the cyclical position jia-wu,
In a corner of the Western sea, in the stagnant waters of the great marsh,
A qilin has in truth been produced, some fifteen feet in height,
Its body that of a deer and with the tail of an ox, with a fleshy horn without bone,
And luminous spots like a red cloud, a purple mist.
Its hooves do not trample upon living creatures and it proceeds with careful tread,
Walking in stately manner and moving in a continuous rhythm.
Its harmonious voice has the sound of a bell or musical tube.
Benevolent is this creature which has appeared but once in all antiquity,
Whose manifestation of divine spirits reaches up to the abode of Heaven.
Ministers and people together vie to be first to gaze upon the joyous spectacle,
As when the Phoenix of Mount Qi sang in the time of Zhou or the River Chart was given to Yu.
The people are united in this year, conforming to the rules of conduct.
Your servant on duty in the Forest of Letters [The Imperial Academy] *who presumed to cherish the ambition to record this event,*
Has chanted this poem to present a hymn of praise to the Sacred Ruler.
Composed by your servant Shen Du, Shi-jiang-xue-shi, Feng-xun-da-fu *of the Academy of Letters.*

In Shen Du's eyes, Emperor Yung Lo had achieved the classical ideal; Heaven and Earth were in harmony; the imperial virtue equalled that of Heaven. The appearance of the *qilin* bore witness to the truth of this belief, to the rightness of those who upheld the Confucian tradition, a select group which included the scholars of the Imperial Academy of Letters.

Modern Myths

According to Kipling:

There are nine and sixty ways of constructing tribal lays
And – every – single – one – of – them – is – right!

What we have seen so far has consisted almost wholly of the constructions of scholars, men who have been concerned to produce stories which will sustain a specific point of view or illustrate a doctrine, lend support to an hypothesis or justify a course of action. Not all such stories belong to the earliest periods of Chinese history: even today stories are being devised or existing tales modified to advocate what are seen to be socially desirable attitudes.

The Prince who Could Not Find a Wife

Eberhard recounts a tale collected in Yunnan by Communist folklorists about a prince who sought a bride and was told by an old man that the best flowers bloom in mountain valleys, the best girls grow up among the common people. 'If you search among the people you will be sure to find a suitable partner.' The quest was unsuccessful, however, because, as the old man explained, goats do not befriend wolves, rats do not marry cats; nor can the common people associate with the son of a king. So the prince hid his identity and lived among the people. The story does not say what happened to the king whose only son he had been.

The Peasant Girl and the Princess

Another story in Eberhard's collection from Yunnan, where it is attributed to the partly sinised I, a Thai tribal group, seems to have been strongly influenced by Communist editing. The girl succeeds when the men are helpless; she sacrifices herself for the community; the king's daughter tacitly admits her superiority although the heroine is of lowly origin. Although poor, she is indifferent to the possibility of wealth. In Eberhard's words, 'practically all these traits run counter to Chinese traditional values'.

There was once a man called Jiao who lived with his daughter near Horse Ear Mountain. The girl was called Sea Girl. In a year of great drought, the people were starving and could not live on their produce, so Jiao and his daughter went up into the mountains to cut bamboos for brooms. One day the daughter saw a shining lake whose waters were wholly clear. Any leaf which fell on to its surface was at once carried off by a great wild goose. Sea Girl took her load of bamboos home and the following day went back with an axe to try to cut a passage from the lake to let the waters into the parched lands of her village. She failed in her attempt, but as she sat in despair under a tree deciding what to do next a wild goose appeared and told her that she needed a golden key to open the lake. Before she could ask where one got a golden key, the goose had gone, and she was forced to ask three parrots who were in the wood where she was how she might obtain such a key. They told her to find the third daughter of the Dragon King.

The girl continued her search until she met a peacock, who advised her that the maiden she sought was to be found in the canyons of the southern mountains. As she set out, the peacock flew ahead of her and was able to tell her that the third daughter of the Dragon King liked the songs

which the people sang. The girl sang folksongs for three days and on the third day, as she sang of the flowers which blossomed on the hillside, the third daughter of the Dragon King appeared, although her father had decreed that no member of his kingdom could enter the human world without specific permission. She admired Sea Girl's singing greatly, for she was a great lover of folksongs, and asked her why she sang and whence she came. The girl explained that she was seeking for the golden key in order to release the waters from the lake for the benefit of the parched fields of her village near Horse Ear Mountain.

The king's daughter told her that the key was in the king's treasury under the guard of an eagle who would kill all comers save the king himself. But one day when the king had left the palace, the girl and the princess sang songs in front of the treasury until the eagle woke and, spreading his wings, came to see who was singing. Then the girl slipped past him and into the treasury. The whole was filled with gold and precious jewels, but these the girl disregarded, seeking only to find the key on which her fellow-villagers' survival depended. She found the key by accident, knocking over a wooden box in which it was hidden, and at once hurried back to the third daughter of the Dragon King. The latter stopped singing and the two girls dashed away to the lake; meanwhile, now that the songs had stopped, the eagle fell asleep again.

Sea Girl used the key to unlock the waters of the lake. There was a great rush of water, and if the Dragon King's daugher had not made her turn off the flow, all the lands of Horse Ear Mountain district would have been disastrously flooded. The girl used straw curtains to stop the threatening flood; these are still there, but the straws have turned to stone. When the Dragon King returned home, he was very angry and banished his daughter, who went to live with Sea Girl and to sing folksongs with her. The women of the district honour them with communal songs on the twenty-second day of the seventh month.

Opposite. Incense burner in the form of a peacock. The peacock was a symbol of beauty and dignity and, according to the Yi, a benefactor of mankind, for he advised Sea Girl how to befriend the daughter of the Dragon King and so unlock the waters. Peacocks also figure among the finds from Shizhaishan, both as free-standing figures and on the bodies of drums. Sixteenth to seventeenth century A.D. Národní Galerie, Prague.

Above. A crane with peaches, symbols of long life, encircled by the *ba gua*, the Eight Precious Things, the Daoist holy symbols. Detail from a funeral surcoat. Early nineteenth century. Victoria and Albert Museum, London.

Chronology of Mythical and Historical Dynasties

	The Three Sovereigns
	Fuxi (also Fuxi/Nugua as divine couple)
	Shennong
	Yan Di
	The Five Emperors
	Huang Di (Yellow Emperor)
	Zhuan Xiu
	Kun
	Yao
	Shun
	Xia Dynasty (Yu to Jie)
*c.*1550-1027 B.C.	**Shang** (Yin) **Dynasty** (Tang to Zhou Xin)
1027-771 B.C.	**Western Zhou**
770-256 B.C.	**Eastern Zhou**
722-480 B.C.	Chun Qiu: Period of the Spring and Autumn Annals
480-221 B.C.	Period of the Warring States
221-207 B.C.	**Qin** (Shi Huang Di, first unifier of China)
202 B.C. - A.D. 9	**Western Han**
9-23	**Interregnum** (Xin Dynasty: Wang Mang)
25-221	**Eastern Han**
221-65	**San Kuo** (Shu Han, Wei, Wu)
265-420	**Jin Dynasty**
420-79	**Song Dynasty**
479-581	**(Six Dynasties)**
581-618	**Sui Dynasty**
618-906	**Tang Dynasty**
907-960	**(Five Dynasties)**
960-1126	**Northern Song Dynasty**
1126-1279	**Southern Song Dynasty**
1260-1368	**Yuan** (Mongol) **Dynasty**
1368-1644	**Ming Dynasty**
1644-1911	**Qing** (Manchu) **Dynasty**
1912-1949	**Republic of China**
1949-	**People's Republic of China**

Further Reading List

Allan, Sarah. *The Heir and the Sage: Dynastic Legend in Early China.* Chinese Materials Center, San Francisco, 1981.
Birch, Cyril. *Chinese Myths and Fantasies.* Oxford University Press, London, 1962.
Bodde, Derk. *Festivals in Classical China.* Princeton University Press, Princeton, 1975. 'Myths of Ancient China'. In S. N. Kramer (ed.) *Mythologies of the Ancient World.* Anchor Books, New York, 1961.
Brewitt-Taylor, C. H. *Romance of the Three Kingdoms.* Kelly & Walsh, Shanghai, 1925.
Chang, Kwang-chih. *Shang Civilization.* Yale University Press, New Haven, 1980.
Christie, Anthony. 'China'. In Richard Cavendish (ed.) *Legends of the World.* Orbis, London, 1982.
Duyvendank, J. J. L. *China's Discovery of Africa.* Probsthain, London, 1949.
Eberhard, Wolfram. *Typen Chinesischer Volksmarchen.* Folklore Fellows Communications, Helsinki, 1937. *Lokalkulturen im Alten China.* T'oung Pao, Leiden, 1943. *Folktales of China.* Routledge & Kegan Paul, London, 1965. *The Local Cultures of South and East China.* Brill, Leiden, 1968.
Forke, Alfred. *Lun-heng.* Paragon, New York, 1962.
Graham, A. C. *The Book of Lieh-tzu.* Murray, London, 1960.
Granet, Marcel. *Danses et Légendes de la Chine ancienne.* Alcan, Paris, 1926. *Festivals and Songs of Ancient China.* (E. D. Edwards, trans.) Routledge, London, 1932. *Chinese Civilisation.* (K. E. Innes & M. R. Brailsford, trans.) Routledge & Kegan Paul, London, 1958. *The Religion of the Chinese People.* (M. Freedman, trans. and ed.) Blackwell, Oxford, 1975.
Hawkes, David. *Ch'u Tz'u: the Songs of the South.* Oxford University Press, Oxford, 1959.
Karlgren, Bernhard. 'Legends and Cults in Ancient China'. *Bulletin of the Museum of Far Eastern Antiquities,* Stockholm 18 (1946), 149-365. 'The Book of Documents'. *B.M.F.E.A.* 22 (1950).
Loewe, Michael. *Ways to Paradise: the Chinese Quest for Immortality.* Allen & Unwin, London, 1979. *Chinese Ideas of Life and Death.* Allen & Unwin, London, 1982.
Maspero, Henri. 'Légendes mythologiques dans le *Chou King*'. *Journal Asiatique* CCIV (1924), 1-100. 'Mythology of Modern China'. In P. L. Couchoud (ed.) *Asiatic Mythology.* Harrap, London, 1932. *Mélanges posthumes sur les Religions et l'Histoire de la Chine,* (3 vols). Civilisations du Sud, Paris, 1950.
Sullivan, Michael. *The Arts of China.* Thames & Hudson, London, 1973.
Waley, Arthur. *The Book of Songs.* Allen & Unwin, London, 1937. *The Nine Songs: a Study of Shamanism in Ancient China.* Allen & Unwin, London, 1955.
Watson, William. *The Genius of China.* Royal Academy, London, 1973.
Werner, Edward T. C. *Myths and Legends of China.* Harrap, London, 1922. *Dictionary of Chinese Mythology.* Kelly & Walsh, Shanghai, 1932.

Acknowledgments

Author's acknowledgments. My interest in Chinese mythology began with a copy of Eve Edwards's translation of Marcel Granet's *Fêtes et Chansons anciennes de la Chine,* bought secondhand when I was still a schoolboy. Further Granet followed, tempered thanks to wise advice, by the more sober and disciplined works of Henri Maspero. Wolfram Eberhard led me further afield in space, time and method. More recently I have benefited from the work of my friends and colleagues: Sarah Allan, a pupil of Eberhard, Angus Graham, Michael Loewe and William Watson. To all of these, as to those many others whose work on this rich material has done so much to increase our understanding, I am deeply grateful. The errors and inadequacies are my own.

Photographic acknowledgments. Art Centrum – Werner Forman 20 left, 25 top, 111 bottom right, 117, 125, 138; Arts Council of Great Britain, London 32, 64–5; Britain-China Friendship Association 89 left; British Museum, London half-title page, 10–11 top, 11, 13, 27, 40, 42–3, 44 left, 57, 78, 82, 85, 88, 93 top, 115, 128; Cleveland Museum of Art, Ohio 76 left, 120, 133; Colour Library International, London 106; Fogg Art Museum, Cambridge, Massachusetts 55 top; Werner Forman Archive, London 36–7, 58; Freer Gallery of Art, Washington D.C. 24; Photographie Giraudon, Paris 45, 64, 121; Richard & Sally Greenhill, London 102, 107; Hamlyn Group Picture Library 7 bottom, 10–11 bottom, 19, 21 left, 25 bottom, 43 right, 46, 54, 55 bottom, 59, 60, 61 right, 62 left, 62 right, 63, 67, 79, 84, 86, 89 right, 100, 104–5, 109, 110, 118, 120–1, 127, 130–1, 134, 135, 139; Robert Harding Picture Library, London frontispiece, 7 top, 12, 18, 20 right, 23 top, 30–1 top, 30–1 bottom, 33, 34, 34–5, 35, 38–9, 50 top, 75, 87, 90, 132–3; Michael Holford, Loughton 103; Mansell Collection, London 80; Bildarchiv Photo Marburg 28, 76 right, 97, 99, 108, 111 top left, 111 top right, 111 bottom left, 129, 130, 131; Metropolitan Museum of Art, New York 42, 49, 53 left, 93 bottom; Minneapolis Institute of Arts, Minnesota 10, 17, 26, 52, 83; Musée Cernuschi, Paris 44 right, 74; Musée Guimet, Paris 22, 47; Museum of Fine Art, Boston, Massachusetts 50 bottom; Museum Rietburg, Zurich 56; Národní Galerie, Prague 71 bottom; National Palace Museum, Taipei 48, 61 left, 65, 71 top, 72, 74–5, 92; William Rockhill Nelson Gallery of Art, Kansas City, Missouri 24–5, 36 top, 36 bottom, 37 top, 37 bottom; Osaka Municipal Museum of Fine Arts 68; Östasiatiska Museet, Stockholm 14, 16; Photoresources, Dover 18–19, 23 bottom, 95; Réalités, Paris 78–9; Seattle Art Museum, Washington 21 right, 43 left, 66, 70, 70–1, 81, 98, 124, 126; Sotheby Parke Bernet, London 128–9; John Massey Stewart, London 119; University of Hong Kong 73, 94, 96; Franco Vannotti, Lugano 29; Wellcome Institute for the History of Medicine, London 53 right; Victoria and Albert Museum, London 77, 91, 108–9, 112, 112–3, 113, 114, 123, 124–5, 132.

Index

References in *italic type* indicate a caption entry.